AMBIGUOUS TERRAINS

An Interspiritual Journey to Judaism

DENISE M. HOFFMAN

BALBOA.
PRESS

A DIVISION OF HAY HOUSE

Balboa Press books may be ordered through booksellers or by contacting:

Balboa Press
A Division of Hay House
1663 Liberty Drive
Bloomington, IN 47403
www.balboapress.com
1 (877) 407-4847

Because of the dynamic nature of the Internet, any web addresses or links contained in this book may have changed since publication and may no longer be valid. The views expressed in this work are solely those of the author and do not necessarily reflect the views of the publisher, and the publisher hereby disclaims any responsibility for them.

The author of this book does not dispense medical advice or prescribe the use of any technique as a form of treatment for physical, emotional, or medical problems without the advice of a physician, either directly or indirectly. The intent of the author is only to offer information of a general nature to help you in your quest for emotional and spiritual well-being. In the event you use any of the information in this book for yourself, which is your constitutional right, the author and the publisher assume no responsibility for your actions.

Any people depicted in stock imagery provided by Thinkstock are models, and such images are being used for illustrative purposes only. Certain stock imagery © Thinkstock.

Print information available on the last page.

ISBN: 978-1-5043-9556-4 (sc)
ISBN: 978-1-5043-9557-1 (hc)
ISBN: 978-1-5043-9582-3 (e)

Library of Congress Control Number: 2018900542

Balboa Press rev. date: 01/12/2018

A NOTE FROM THE AUTHOR

In the Siddur (prayer book of Reform Judaism), there is a poignant, powerful meditation that speaks of destiny. Here it is in its entirety:

> Once or twice in a lifetime, a man or woman may choose a radical leaving, having heard Lech-l'cha-Go forth. God disturbs us towards our destiny by hard events and by freedom's now urgent voice ... which explodes and confirms who we are. We don't like leaving ... but God loves becoming. (Reform Siddur, *Mishkan T'Filah*, p. 113)

When I first contemplated this meditation, images of balls of light, originating in the celestial ethers, came front and center. A journey from one realm of existence to another begins time and again. The purpose will ultimately be revealed, yet in all likelihood, it has to do with manifesting one's divine purpose here on planet Earth.

On deeper reflection, however, I also began to wonder if this meditation held a clue as to why we, collectively as a human species, seem to thrive on what is comfortable, familiar, and rational. Is it because, on the deepest of levels, we have experienced leaving the familiarity of one realm and going to the unfamiliarity of another?

None of these earthly journeys have followed any specific linear pattern, and as to be expected, those sparks have certainly gotten muddied along the way, sometimes even obscured. At times, many of us have wondered if perhaps we were misfiled destination-wise.

In the Jewish mystical writings, there is a precedent for this. The term *gilgul* refers to a soul that was somehow separated from Judaism and eventually found itself living a life quite different from what was originally intended. Upon recognition (in many cases, that recognition culminates in formal conversion), the soul returns to the practice of Judaism.

In describing the gilgul, the term *misfiled* (and there have been many other similar terms used as well) in reference to the soul has often been used. But what if the soul was never really misfiled to begin with? Since the mystical writings of many diverse spiritual traditions/practices are often onion layered, could the word misfiled be another term for reincarnation, as well as remembering our true identities as spiritual immigrants having human experiences? In the Kabbalistic writings, reincarnation is often described as the means for which a soul incarnates for the purpose(s) of completing a Tikkun (loosely translated as correction, repair). And since many writings from diverse sources also speak of inclusiveness, expansiveness, and caring for the marginalized other, could the gilgul actually represent the experiential dimension of being that, upon transformation of one's self, leads to an elevation of one's consciousness? When time reveals itself to be, can someone who has embodied such an experience return to share what has been learned?

This is where my journey begins again ... and anew.

Five years ago, one journey began with the first and only meeting of my birth mother and sisters. This journey, as it would later be revealed, was the catalyst that would come to transform a narrow bridge into a more expansive and evolving one. In the process, it empowered me to seek the home in Judaism that had been resonating within for the longest time ... a subtle yet powerful resonation. As one journey began to evolve into another, it became clear to me that both of these significant journeys were part of an even more significant, evolving, and interconnected journey—that being the journey toward evolving consciousness.

That journey, which involves remembering who one really is and living from that place, is what speaks to me in the words of the meditation, "But God loves becoming."

People convert to religions for a variety of reasons, and even those considered most common (i.e., marriage, giving the family a clear religious identity, seeking a new spiritual home) don't come close to describing that which can never be fully explained by the cause-and-effect reasoning so prevalent in our culture. The few people I chose to open up to and share this life-changing event (reunion) with could not understand how a reunion could ultimately destabilize one's world as one knows it, which is exactly what this pivotal event did. From this destabilization, I sought a new spiritual home (which wasn't really new, as I had grown up in an interfaith background with religious diversity, something I grew to respect and cherish). I could understand their rationalizations, even as I began to realize that much of it was, sad to say, fear based. From the telltale moment that I set my eyes on my birth mother and sisters, I tried as best I could (a moment full awe, gratitude, and shock) to be in a moment that had no reasoning to it. What I was experiencing would appear threatening to many people and for many reasons, most notably because it tossed the applecart of what "should" have happened (i.e., mothers don't relinquish their children) and what "should" now result from this experience (i.e., happily ever after now once reunited ... not exploring spiritual practices!). I had no way of knowing that eight months later, I would contact an interspiritual rabbi to seek his advice on how to grow from that experience, or that in another two months, I would be sitting in front of the rabbi who would eventually preside over my conversion ceremony another four years later. Having also awakened to the energetic, empathic side of my nature (which explained many things, most notably around absorbing chaotic energies both physically and emotionally in crowded, noisy places, something I could never understand while growing up) and having become more grounded within it, I surrendered my need to know and learned to trust the guidance leading me in a new direction, whether it made sense or not.

As the journeys continued, and as I became more grounded in my energy practices (a work in progress), I began to practice discernment in regard to with whom I shared my journeys. There was much sacred space opening up, and some things were to be known only by me.

A new course was about to be charted, but before that could happen, I needed to discover what caused me to go off course in the beginning.

And that was where it started ... in the beginning. With a set of false beliefs about who I was, predicated on the early life experience of relinquishment, subsequent false patterns would follow. It was this pattern, as well as absorbing toxic cultural views, that caused my separation from the masculine, feminine, and transcendent aspects of the divine. Yet, with much inner work, explosive at times, the spark that had once been obscured started to shine, and the lotus began to fully blossom.

I also began to see, via explorative study, that themes of relinquishment, adoption, and reunion, not given much thought in mainstream religions, were a lot more common than I had realized. In fact, many of those who are hailed as master teachers/sages from a variety of spiritual traditions have, in fact, experienced some of these themes in their own lives. That alone convinced me that what I and many others in the adoption constellation had experienced was not separate from the whole. When I stepped out of the "I, me, and mine" mantra (which at some point has to happen), I began to see that the illusory shadow sides of ownership, erroneously believing that one person can be replaced with another, and unresolved grief issues surrounding the above-mentioned themes have been part of a drama that has been playing itself out repeatedly, and sometimes destructively, for centuries on the global stage.

Yet a newly emerging stage revealed that the adoption and reunion experience, diverse as it is, held within it the seeds of service, not subservience, to all.

Judaism had called out to me. Its message, accompanied by shofars and Sinai thunder, was actually very subtle but not less powerful:

> You must sanctify yourself by releasing the baggage that you have accumulated throughout all of your life experiences, and that have distorted your vision. Free of such distortions, you will again see the wisdom of such experiences purpose-wise. For in order for Tikkun Olam to manifest within the world, it must first be experientially manifest within oneself.
>
> Consciousness elevating wisdom comes from all walks of life. Remember, learn, and grow from that.

A journey such as the one I was now embarking on, as well as the mini-journeys within, is often, by its very nature, difficult to articulate. Nonetheless, this taking charge of spirit journey has been divided into four parts: "Separation," "The Dark Night of the Soul," "Light," and "Appreciation," as described by Dr. Caroline Myss (www.myss.com). For symbolically creative purposes, these parts are described as bridges, with a power animal at the entrance to offer sage advice.

In "Separation," all of the falseness surrounding my life experiences, including but not limited to the reunion experience, is exposed. In reclaiming that original spark, relinquishment of that which was no longer conducive to purpose of being begins. Symbolically speaking, this is when the world as one knows it begins to crumble.

"The Dark Night of the Soul" is a descent into the shadows, including a confrontation of them, when one realizes that nothing will ever be the same again. This is where the many fantasies I had harbored about the reunion being a happily-ever-after experience had to die. It was also where I had to come to terms with the reality that the only person I was ever responsible for healing was myself. I learned what was mine to transform and what was not mine to transform. It was also the place where a new, more expansive image of the Creator would eventually take formless form, once the old throne God, who alternately hurled thunderbolts of rewards and punishments, was permanently expunged from consciousness.

In "Light," much of the necessary darkness of the previous stage gave way to increasing shards of illumination. I physically felt myself becoming lighter. Yet, at times, this stage was also the most painful, as I realized that the ones closest to me whom I had called friends were no longer around. Sad as I was, however, I could not look back.

Finally, there was appreciation for all that had evolved. I became more fully present in my body and learned to listen to its wisdom, especially when it came to play (a message I'm sure many of us hear and debate whether or not to listen to—hopefully we will choose to listen!). In addition, as I became more present, I was able to take steps to honor what was to be honored, embrace what was to be embraced, and, in time and with practice, relinquish attachments to any particular outcome, grateful for all that had happened. In seeing with evolving eyes, I was also able to be more authentically compassionate and less reactionary in diverse environmental surroundings. All this growth took place while journeying to the spiritual home awaiting me.

None of these interconnected journeys has ever been about being perfect. Other than the certainty that we are far more powerful than we have imagined and that we are responsible for healing ourselves, I make no claims. Each of us must find our jewels in the lotus and dust them off, because we are those jewels that are meant to shine.

It is my wish, dear readers, that while reading *Ambiguous Terrains: An Interspiritual Journey to Judaism*, you encounter these writings with an open and engaging heart (which does not mean agreeing with everything). As stated, I make no claims, yet if somewhere in these writings you come to remember who you have always been, then I am profoundly grateful for having been granted this opportunity.

May your journeys be blessed.

Shalom/Namaste,
Denise M. Hoffman

ALEGRIA

Alegria (joy) had been looking for a nameless name and the energy it represented. Oh, she had many names, but these names, though initially valuable, had obscured a nameless name deep within her that sought release. A name that, like a caterpillar that turns into a butterfly, would turn a child into a woman. She would be released from the ties that bound her gentle and wild nature, all the while realizing that a nameless name represented a much greater vastness that words could convey.

A snake charmer waited at the first bridge. The closer Alegria came, the more the cobra began to dance and sway like a goddess to the haunting melodies vibrating from the pipe. Keeping respectful distance, Alegria could see old skins, signs of shedding. Then, without warning, the cobra turned in her direction and spat potent venom. The target was her eyes, and the venom burned through her protective glasses, blinding her to what she perceived as reality.

"You must begin to see the world with new eyes," hissed the cobra. After being momentarily stunned, Alegria opened her still-burning eyes and saw only darkness. Somehow, though, she managed to step onto a single-footed, narrow bridge.

SEPARATION

Time to start cutting some umbilical cords, lest you be strangled by them.

From a symbolic perspective, *reunion*, paradoxically, would come to mean separation. The umbilical cords of attachment that follow us from one realm of existence to another, though possibly helpful, can become chains of oppression when we believe that it is the chains themselves (i.e., our stories about who we think we are) that ground us in the earthly realm rather than our essences. There is a timeless wisdom that says what is seen on the outside is but a reflection of what exists within. Preceding this pivotal event was a medical trip to Nicaragua, a destabilizing hurricane, a series of "accidental" deaths, the release of a long-held trauma, the closure of my former high school, and the death of a religion teacher whose presence, inside and outside of the classroom, had been aligned with both talking and walking the walk. All of these happenings severed umbilical cord attachments and closed one chapter of my life as I knew it.

Although I went on with everyday life, deep down I knew that what was happening externally was also happening internally.

Something was preparing to come into being as something else was preparing to fade away.

Yet what was coming into being would be concealed for quite some time—until the time was right for it to be revealed.

So what happened on that surreal day so long ago when I met my birth mother and sisters for the first time?

Happily shocked though I was during that blur of a twenty-four-hour period, there was a part of me that remained outside of it all. Call it merging with eagle consciousness. The subtle message I got was this: "Yes, there is a seventh presence here, as you have intuited. As you have always been guided, you are now being guided into new terrains. Cherish and grieve this moment simultaneously, for it will never again come in this plane of existence. Prepare to let go."

Naturally, that was not a subtle message likely to be well received by any member of the adoption constellation participating in a reunion!

Nonetheless, I sensed all along that this would be a onetime event. I could see the bigger picture. Still, I struggled with what was evolving, most notably in the cause-and-effect arena. After all, I had spent much time and effort reading, researching, and connecting both personally and through emails with professionals who understood the complexities of such an experience. Did I seek to be rewarded for my efforts? Of course! My cup was overflowing with so much information that there was hardly any space to welcome whatever was to be poured.

There is a wonderful Zen story about a seeker who is interested in studying with a renowned master. During the interview with the student, the master listens patiently to the student talk incessantly about his studies and experiences (which reminds me of my converting rabbi who, God bless her, listened with great equanimity—not to mention patience—to my overflowing stories!). The master starts to pour a cup of tea, and the student eventually pauses from his dissertations long enough to see the overflowing cup. He yells for the master to stop pouring. "The cup is overflowing!" cries the student. The master then replies, "And so are you. How can I teach you anything?" (Lama Surya Das, *Awakening to the Sacred*, p. 43).

I've often wondered if the student in the above story was caught in cause-and-effect thinking because, on some level, welcoming something new, no matter how much desired, might have been threatening to his sense of self. Perhaps he too wished to be rewarded for all of his spiritual efforts. In this particular scenario, the quest was for healing and for developing a more consciously connected compassion to those closest to me. And from a bleeding-heart perspective, I wanted to have the dream come true of all of my families coming together (a common inner wish, I strongly intuit, of many who were part of the closed adoption system of the yesteryears). The first two were cultivatable and sustainable. The third one, as I would come to realize, was not. I could, however, do my part to heal whatever rifts I had created in my relationships by being unaware and making unconscious choices. Somewhere down the road, I would come to learn more about the energies of detachment and discernment, and I would put them into practice when it came to owning my issues and not taking on someone else's.

Bottom line: I wanted to be both the pourer of the tea and the cup that received its contents!

Before I go any further, I wish to state that seeking and exploring are part and parcel of any transformational journey. I also wish to state that what we wish to seek, for the most part, has always been within. As a species, we are a lot more powerful than we have understood ourselves to be, and it is useless to expect others to do our inner work for us. Part of what I was doing was moving to a place of empowerment not previously recognized within myself. The conflicts arose when insights from the combined practices of yoga, meditation, and breath work revealed that the origin of what needed to be transformed did not originate on the academic plane of existence. Its origins were spiritual.

In my first book, *Ocultando No Mas / Hiding No More: Unmasking Adoption and Reunion* (Rosedog Books 2009), I likened the reunion to an individual crossing a bridge that leads to a new phase of existence and that, upon looking back, disintegrates. This is similar to the biblical story of Sodom and Gomorrah, when Lot's wife looks back at the destruction and turns into a pillar of salt. There are many diverse interpretations here. Allegorically speaking, could one of those themes speak about not getting stuck in the past and instead living in the present? Like the cobra at the beginning of this chapter, could this tale be speaking of the creation of new being balanced with destruction of old? Could this tale also be speaking of healing the earth?

I also began to realize, with a heavy heart, that to welcome an evolving new phase of life, the bridge of the catalytic event known as reunion would at some point have to be destroyed as well.

This was, to say the least, difficult to process—especially since I am a sponge for surrounding energies. This was not about destroying people, though I was well aware that this would be painful. What was being destroyed, I hoped, was any and all attachments of feeling like I needed to be defined solely by this experience as well as by the insidious need to be right about it. There was no way to predict outcomes, though through centering practices of compassion, discernment, and detachment, clarity would eventually reveal itself. And speaking of revelation, so would new teachers eventually reveal themselves, most of whom were not connected with adoption and reunion.

While there was an internal uprooting occurring, there was an external one as well. As someone who embodied a mosaic of colorful birth heritages as a mixed-race Latina and who also had wonderful adoption experiences, I noticed subtle shifts of awareness in that I was no longer interested in identifying myself solely as this type of linear thought pattern so common in Western culture. This did not mean that I was not proud of my earthly roots. I was. It just meant that I was reuniting with the reality that I was more than what appeared on the surface. Yet I found myself more interested in exploring the spiritual wisdoms and lore that were part of these heritages. In time, I would become even more interested in learning how such wisdoms could be applied in cocreating a higher level of awareness.

I also found my awareness starting to shift when I talked about the reunion itself. Since many people have asked me what it's like to have an adoption experience—and make no mistake, it's not a one-size-fits-all experience—I found myself enjoying the role of teacher in providing explanations. Sometimes I enjoyed the role a bit too much! I was indeed grateful for the friends who stood by me during this time, and also, at times, I was troubled. Perhaps the question I needed to ask myself was whether or not I was sharing or teaching out of a need to be right and a need to blame rather than doing so from a place of centeredness. The years of having to field insensitive questions, though necessary for learning how to proactively stand up for myself, had taken their toll. The years of trying to explain myself in the hopes of fitting in external boxes had not always left me feeling like I was in a good place emotionally. Grateful though I was to be living in a country of material abundance, I was also tired of fielding arrogant remarks about how different life would have been had I been raised in Latin America. It had been in my heart to try to understand that those remarks were not always made out of spite but perhaps out of a person's knowing only one such way of life that followed a linear pattern. Nonetheless, such remarks needed to be challenged. Well intended and not well intended, such rationalizations revealed that some surrounding me were indeed uncomfortable with what I was facing. The limits of cause-and-effect thinking might not be bursting only my bubble. The challenge here was to acknowledge what was emerging without projecting it onto anyone else. I was, by far, not the only one who was hurting. In time, what had felt so good in terms of my own validation ultimately felt anything but good. I started to wish that the ones I called my friends would kick me to the curb and out of a limited and limiting mind-set. Of course, they could not, because that was to be my sacred task. Service, not subservience, to others was what was emerging from the depths within when it came to the adoption/reunion experience, as was impermanence.

Impermanence is the proverbial elephant in the room that no one likes to acknowledge, yet is always there. A reunion can give one the ability to transform numerous tissue issues that arise, because, at some point, either on the earthly realm of existence, saying goodbye to one way of living, or via death, the experience will have to be relinquished once again. This was what was now arising in my consciousness.

Cause-and-effect, reward-and-punishment perspectives were in the process of being disbanded. As someone who has spent most of her working life in the health professions (first as a cardiac technician and then as a personal trainer), I began to pick up on some energetic vibrations that had been previously dormant, making themselves known via electrical disturbances at times. When working with new clients, I could intuit many things even before they spoke. Naturally, I kept these things to myself, as it was more important to engage in meaningful dialogue than to speak for someone else. I had dismissed what was going on, despite the fact that I was now becoming ever more aware of how sensitive I had always been to atmospheric changes that could not be described with words. Watches never lasted on me for very long. These changes were both people-wise and weather-wise. Even though I had experienced these inner workings throughout my own life, I was not yet ready to give full credence to the mind-body-spirit connection—even though I had spent a good part of graduate school studying such connections (again, this was on an academic level; the experiential had arrived and was yet to come) and observing such connections being practiced while in Nicaragua! Loving-kindness was a more potent healer than any drug could offer. What I was seeing there was the embodiment of the phrase "made in the divine image," and even more so, in likeness.

As someone who was initially schooled in Western ideology, I can say that I am more than grateful for its innovations and that such innovations, health-wise, have contributed to the vast improvements of many lives the world over. Yet during this time, I also began to see the limits of such innovations as well. Not everything can be fixed with a pill. My studies had initially focused on fixing, almost to the exclusion of making reference to the body's innate healing wisdom. Cultivating patterns of conscious eating, stress management, exercise, rest, and generosity went far beyond height-weight charts. It was about the whole person, from the inside out. Nothing was separate, as I had originally been taught. It was all interconnected. The questions I pondered in time with regard to one's lifestyle evolved around questions as to what fuels a healthy lifestyle and what causes imbalance. I finally came to accept both as energetic in origin and, in all likelihood, the result of not always being physically present in the physical body. This in no way discounted genetic and lifestyle choices. It was just another piece of the puzzle.

Truth be told, none of these shifts in awareness were comfortable. In fact, they were downright aggravating! As an avid independent film buff, I found myself increasingly bored by what I was watching on the screen. As important as it was to be aware of all of the suffering in the world, it was equally important not to be drained by it. This did not equate to denial, but it did mean becoming more aware of the movies I watched, the foods I ate, and even to some degree the company I kept. I was becoming allergic to life as I once knew it, and this was reflected in minor health disturbances. Situations and people that sapped vitality, and that included my own energy-sapping ways, were limited. I was no longer interested in the misery-loves-company mantra. Instead, I was more interested in being part of life-enhancing vibrations and living and teaching from that place.

This also meant cultivating more playfulness and keeping grounded in what was occurring in each moment. When that happened, the so-called ordinary became extraordinary. The words of my favorite songs now took on a deeper meaning, as if to say, "Pay attention. I'm talking to you."

Still, there were more bridges to cross. If compassion could be cultivated for people in distant lands, why was it such a challenge for me here sometimes? It appeared that the cup that had runneth over now had made space for something else to take formless form.

That formless form was this: if the origin of what was happening was spiritual, and I no longer doubted that it was, what did this say about the Creator and any perspectives that needed to be revisited and possibly relinquished?

Alegria had been shaky on her feet when she began and was now even more so as she approached the second bridge. The first one had been shaped like a mountain that, to the untrained eye, appeared to be easy to climb. Alegria's eyes, however, having been infused by the spitting cobra, found navigating this ambiguous terrain a challenge like no other.

Of course, she didn't realize what was coming up next!

Nothing about crossing the first bridge had been surefooted. Nonetheless, she had managed to stumble her way through the overgrown thickets, some of which obscured the sparkling radiance of the tallest of trees, and found herself standing a few feet away from the second bridge.

If one could even call this contraption a bridge!

It was wooded, rusty, and held together by ropes resembling spaghetti noodles, but what appeared most striking to Alegria were the cobwebs!

Was she really supposed to be crossing a bridge that, on first sight, seemed to go nowhere? The only sights that she could make out were smoke-covered clouds. Upon second glance, it appeared that those smoke-covered clouds were expanding out to include the lower rock formations of the river below.

Upon third sight, however, Alegria saw a mutant-looking tortoise slowly creeping toward the cobweb-infested bridge. Somewhere in the deep recesses of her awareness, the old story of the tortoise and the hare emerged. The slow-as-molasses tortoise, perhaps seeing that the journey and the destination were one and the same, and not getting attached to a specific outcome, completed its task. On the other hand, its outer shell seemed to protect it from the slings and darts of life. Was it possible that such protection could also be too restrictive at times? Could the tortoise be carrying too much on its shoulders of a shell?

In observing the tortoise, was she projecting onto the tortoise what she had been carrying and longed to set down … without turning over?

Another powerful insight emerged: perhaps the shell housing the tortoise's essence represented interconnected reality as well as the reality that this animal was quite grounded on all levels.

Alegria watched as the tortoise slowly and methodically made its way to the center of the unstable bridge, barreling through the cobwebs as if on a mission. Then, surprisingly, the tortoise withdrew into its shell. Taking carefully measured steps across the now-swaying bridge, Alegria was now in close reach of touching the tortoise. Maybe if she could gently …

Then, without warning, the tortoise fell through a bridge slat and descended into the unknown depths below!

Alegria was shocked. What was the meaning of such an abrupt departure? Was she supposed to rescue the tortoise?

The winds were now whipping all around her. Looking down, she gasped in astonishment as she saw the tortoise rise from the waters and eventually disappear into a cave, an opening that she hadn't noticed before. She could not tell what lay beyond that opening. She could, however, tell that the tortoise, shell and all, moved much less encumbered than before.

And that's when Alegria's bridge slat gave way, and she, like the tortoise before her, fell.

THE DARK NIGHT OF THE SOUL

*Note to readers: This particular section involves lessons being taught, and subsequently revealed, to the author by none other than her shadow. The author's download of perspectives will follow. All that is required in this moment is that judgment of any and all kind be suspended.

"Everything reveals itself in time." Hmmm ... that's a cryptic message if I ever heard one (and I did, in an email from your rabbi).

Cryptic ... and true in the sense that it is now time to fully reveal myself to you.

I don't have any particular name, though I have been endlessly named by humanity for centuries. Yet since I am revealing myself to you for the first time, and since you appear to love the lyrical (an inheritance from your Latin American ancestors), I will refer to myself as Sombra, which means shadow.

More specifically ... your shadow.

Yes, I am aware that, linguistically, Sombra has different meanings based on the context in which it is used. Perhaps *oscuridad* would serve the grammatically picky. I am not here, however, to serve the grammatically picky. The hourglass has been turned upside down, which means time is really of the essence. Please note the significance of the last word in the previous sentence.

Now let's get down to business!

First of all, you have had some big-time misgivings about the nefarious shadow. Yet what many don't realize is that I am not something outside of you. I reside within, always have and always will. The cosmos is a mixture of dark and light. This interplay, appearing chaotic at times, is what brings creation into existence. The cosmos exists within. You are not separate from the whole, as you and countless others have erroneously believed. Such misgivings have led to centuries of violence of unprecedented proportions, often spurred by focusing the finger outward while forgetting to acknowledge the fingers pointing inward, meaning—individually and collectively—you!

Like many before you, and until very recently, you were too afraid to look at your own darkness, which means you have been unconsciously acting it out. You have been afraid of what it can teach you. And why is that? Because the collective conditioning of your time has stated that darkness must be banished at all costs. It has ignored wholeness of all interconnected aspects of the self. This warlike approach has failed to take into account that that which is dark on the outside is merely a reflection of what is dark within. Put simply, what you don't own, you project.

And since our time here is short, I will give you a few perspectives from one who has been a perennial insider looking out ... and sometimes vice versa.

The biggest leap of faith you took in trying to look within at your own darkness was via contacting that interfaith rabbi eight months ago after that catalytic, and yes, cataclysmic rite of passage known as reunion. It went against the grain of conventional common sense. After all, those surrounding you wondered, how could such an event change one's perspective of what is known as God? (Yes, your experience and the fact that you let yourself be battered by ambiguous winds without needing cause-and-effect explanations, and seeing some semblance of order behind the mask of chaos was threatening some of your closest friends.) Talk about surprised! He was to be the beginning of a new set of teachers you would be welcoming in your continual evolution and shedding of the past. Because his response was so on the mark, I will repeat it here:

"Now about this notion that 'I am trying to shed an ego that I now realize was there to protect me from being left again, as I was at birth.' Who is the you that is trying to shed the ego? This is like trying to hear your own ears. You are that protective ego, and you are so much more than that. I try not to shed anything and make room for everything. That ego had its place. Honor it even as you grow so much larger than it as to make its protection unnecessary. And the best way, as you have said, is through meditation, yoga, and service to others. Work to deepen your centeredness in God (reality, Tao, etc.) and engage your life with compassionate curiosity. I hope this helps a little bit."

And to think that you almost let fear of what somewhat else would say about your scenario stop you from receiving such a stellar response!

When was the last time you were compassionate and merciful toward yourself for all of your real and imagined shortcomings? Wholeness is not about being perfect. It never was. From an ancestral and cultural perspective, you have allowed yourself to absorb too much toxicity, mistakenly believing that taking on the woes of others was the compassionate and merciful response. And what did that get you? A solar plexus screaming in agony and numerous panic attacks. This is when you started to awaken to the reality that part of your graduate studies in alternative health / energy medicine was more than just academic; it was experiential. So you did the responsible thing and finally had your blocked nasal septum surgically corrected and thus became calmer, growing in awareness of what belongs to you and what does not. Why was this? Because you had now connected to both sides of your breath. Unless someone is about to fall down a manhole or step on a rattlesnake, a compassionate person does not rescue or save another person from one's own life. Though well intentioned, did it ever occur to you that such interference might be taking away another's free will, maybe even on a cosmic level? Being in the moment with the suffering soul, while remaining detached, is what compassion is all about. I know that this goes against the grain of what you have been taught and conditioned to think, but energetically, you know this to be true. As an empath, you truly embody the experience of the other, literally, in that you know how it feels to be in another's shoes, which is all the more reason to practice detachment instead of always leaving an opening for attachment. Again and again, you have had a hard time learning this, which is why I have had to pull the rug repeatedly out from under you.

Look more closely at the phrase, "You are that protective ego ... and you are so much more than that. That ego had its place. Honor it as you grow so much larger than it as to make its protection unnecessary." So much more than that, and you still doubt your magnificence at times! How very silly! Whether you realize it or not, you are a creation of that interconnected dance between dark and light. Note the words "protective ego" and, more specifically, "had its place." This is significant in that *had* is past tense, which means it's time to let go of much of the overprotectiveness that has characterized your life. Make a note here: this does not mean dropping boundaries. It simply means living in the here and now. Whether such overprotectiveness was a result of prior challenging incarnations or the present one, this behavior has been largely learned, which means it can and must be unlearned. I can tell you right now: you have been a lot stronger than you have allowed yourself to admit, and such protectiveness was only supposed to be for a short period of time. It was never supposed to be 24/7, which eventually becomes constrictive, as in no air supply. You have wanted to shed an ego without fully understanding and, in some ways, experiencing what a healthily developed ego is all about.

So, I'll tell you. It's about transformation. Transforming your ego to be in service to your soul, not the other way around.

And, indeed for you, this is a continuing moment of transformation.

Do you really want to know about the stumbling blocks that have kept you from experiencing your full potential? Does the story of Sampson and Delilah ring a bell here? There is much untapped wisdom in this centuries-oldie-but-goodie biblical story, which goes much deeper than Delilah being scorned as a villainess. Truth be told, a soul does not evolve without challenges, which end up being the greatest of teachers.

This brings me to the word "centeredness."

How can one be centered in Source if one is putting anything and anyone before the Creator? Could the word jealous, often mentioned in biblical writings and interpreted literally through the human lens, actually mean something far more indescribable? If the Creator can be likened to a waterfall that flows through the land, then can jealous be a code word meaning that if every relationship on earth flows, it must first flow from the Source? Perhaps a more apropos word would be aligned. It is impossible to receive when one is full of oneself or is always putting up barriers to such reception. Idolatry is, in its basic sense, putting anything before God. If you ever owned that draconian perspective about statues, get rid of it right now! People today are not bowing down to the Buddha. They are bowing down to BMWs! In the grander scheme of things, we own nothing. This, among many arenas, includes what is called "woundedness." When one puts the battle scars from life experiences (which were pre-chosen before incarnation for soul growth and mending purposes) before the Creator, it is akin to saying that the power of woundedness, which can only thrive if one continually feeds it, is stronger than the power to heal, transform, and create. Holding on to such scars blocks the divine energy one is meant to receive and share. This was one of the reasons that, upon publication of your first book and its sequel, and after becoming involved with adoption activism for open records, you felt so lost. All those years of not knowing such basic information and the suffering you and your family experienced led you to the conclusion that someone should pay. At that moment, you were experiencing the human emotion of revenge. You were taking your reunion experience that was full of teaching wisdom and using it punitively. This was the action part of your purpose of being, and you misused your power deeply. And not only did you misuse your power, you felt it as well ... like being punched in the gut!

Face it : you are too energetically sensitive for engaging in such toxic behavior. This is the energetic version of what goes around comes around, not punishment but consequence. No matter how mad you get, the idea of intentionally hurting someone, even in necessary self-defense, sickens you to your stomach. When mentioning your activism to a medical intuitive, also a reunited birth mother, she immediately picked up on the fact that you were filtering your reunion experience via the lens of revenge. You chose not to stay there. This particular teacher taught you about the dangers of letting toxic emotions simmer, especially for sensitives and empaths. Actually, it is no good for anyone. From this teacher, you started to take the initial steps in learning to trust your intuition more than you had in earlier times.

And speaking of activism, when intentions are aligned with actions, activism is, in and of itself, sacred. Perfection is not, nor has it ever been, required to participate. Nevertheless, the shadow sides of activism are numerous, most notably when one believes that the cause is more about oneself rather than the cause itself. This is not what activism, at its core, is about. It's about addressing injustices from a place of compassionate detachment without needing to punish anyone. You didn't initially start out with such a punitive mind-set; you just let yourself become spellbound by what was going on around you, and within you as well. Take it from me: people who commit acts of injustice suffer far more than many realize, and it's not your place to render judgment. The energy that it takes to hold such heavy burdens is enormous, and it's energy that could be channeled into more creative purposes. Earth judgment is one thing. Eternal judgment is quite another, and it's best left in the hands of the Creator.

You have will. Never doubt that. You always have and always will. However, you have not always been keenly aware of how to channel that will consistently. It's time to take higher aim, which you cannot accomplish without being grounded spiritually. That is the other reason you have had a hard time acknowledging, let alone celebrating, the accomplishments that have been part of your chosen experience all along. Do you wish to know why you have floundered in this arena? Because you have been far too much of a student and have not balanced that role with that of a teacher. That's right! It's time to be your own guru and not anyone else's. Just as you have been gently turned away from latching on to another's perspectives, so too must you now return the favor when someone appears to be latching on to your perspectives without doing the necessary work of introspection. This does not mean that you will not be a student anymore. Life is, after all, a learning and remembering journey. But you, along with many others, have had this, I would call, fervent need to give away your personal power to anyone who bears the title of "religious."

That's pure insanity ... and yes, idolatry. How can any external force know what the song of your soul is? Can one know what someone else's soul song is? The only one to know is the one whose soul lives within. You didn't trust your compass that spoke to the above when confronted. Why? Because belonging felt safer than listening to your gut. Don't blame those who steered you in useless directions. You allowed it. Blame is useless. In fact, it has been your so-called adversaries who have taught you more spiritually than the sweet, sentimental ones.

Yet, without a doubt, probably the most overlooked form of idolatry is one that is so obvious and yet so overlooked. The false god of fear.

You have known fear within yourself and also from absorbing the fears of those surrounding you. My question here is this: have you ever known its opposite—love? This is internal, as you have known it, since it was from this breath that the universe came to be (that means you!). It is an unconditional love that surpasses any conditionality. You have not, at times, experientially understood this, though you are starting to remember this now. Because of this, you have felt ungrounded. Isn't it time to experience groundedness? Titles come and go, but the infinite is eternal. You have experienced many God-centered moments in your life, mostly when it involved service to others. The question at this very moment is this: has your perspective on the Creator evolved?

Remember this: one cannot really mature without maturing spiritually.

And while we are on the subject of the Creator, I will shed a little light on some shadows you have had. Bear with me, as some of what is being expressed dances between the particular and the universal.

First off, the phrase "made in the image and likeness of God." Esoterically speaking, we are all beings of light, which is a noun, though, in some respects, possibly a verb as well. The likeness aspect represents choice, which is a verb. Do we choose to see the divine image in all ... even those whose actions may appear less than divine? Do we choose to engage each moment proactively or reactively? Those are the questions. Form and formless. How we answer is, as always, up to us, both individually and collectively.

If this takes your breath away, then you are just beginning to understand a whole new way of being that might eventually involve a shift away from the human laws of cause and effect. When you symbolically look at yourself as a spark of the divine, you can never look at anything in the same light again.

Powerful stuff.

And while we are on the subject of idolatry and the Creator, it would serve you well to transcend any and all archaic perspectives that refer to the Creator as one who rewards and punishes. Humans do this. The Creator never does. Projecting human qualities onto the Creator has caused more bloodshed than can ever be imagined. Closer to home, this reunion experience has made you realize that you have been projecting both sets of parents onto the Creator. Forgiveness, generosity, compassion, detachment, mercy, and love are not just a mere few aspects of the Creator. They are the Creator. Nonetheless, even realizing that, it is also known that the essential nature of the Creator can never be fully known. Putting human qualities on the Creator is putting a face on that which is clearly not human.

Want some up-to-date perspectives on "graven images"? How about the image that says that you are a helpless, hapless soul, all alone, and that nothing you do will make a difference? How about the image of the conqueror, whose mantra, most likely originating from a scarcity mind-set, says that there is never enough and hoards so that what is obtained will not be taken away? If this isn't arousing, then how about images suggesting that the Creator plays favorites? Another version of this might be parroted as "My god is better than your god." And my favorite: images that suggest that the earth is a useless plaything. These are just but a few, and what connects them? Fear.

And speaking of agendas, relinquish the idea that the Creator must bow down to structured constructs of what we imagine He/She/It to be. The spiritual realm of cause and effect operates quite differently. Sometimes, infants and children do indeed die before their parents. You have closely witnessed this in your own life. Life is ambiguous and does not necessarily conform to our timetable. In fact, as someone who has lived an adoption experience from the closed adoption system from the yesteryears, you are living proof of not only ambiguity but that cause and effect isn't always, well, cause and effect as is viewed by conventional thought.

And on this topic of relinquishment, relinquish the childish notion of ever thinking that this reunion experience was about *one happily ever after, big, happy family on all sides* scenario. It is simply not a vibrational match, and the journey you are now embarking on is.

My time is running out, and I have given you much to contemplate. Nonetheless, I will leave you with a few more tips. While you are picking up the pieces of your shattered vessel, remember that a spark shines best when it lives in the present moment. When you remember that, my so-called protection will be useless. Get rid of any and all traces of sentimentality, which is another block to the here and now. Work to use you time and energy differently and walk away from that which is not sustainable. Step back from habitual reactivity, and in those moments of solar plexus queasiness, ask yourself, "Is this mine or someone else's?"

Above all, take time to play. It's really not that serious!

Hmmm ... maybe there is a method to this madness.

I'll be watching you all right, with one hand on the rug on which you stand, just in case you need a little reminding.

This was quite a download. While I knew that I had all the time in the world to resolve what needed to be resolved, I also knew, from the way the world was spinning, that there was some sense of inexplicable urgency. I no longer cared about explaining it. I just wanted now to be with it.

"Has your perspective on the Creator evolved?"

It would have been tempting to respond with the sarcastic, juvenile pattern of "Evolved from what?" but that time period and those response patterns were long over.

Had it evolved from the culturally ingrained image of the

Creator as being a savior, rescuer, and throne God who alternated between hurling thunderbolts of rewards and punishments?

Not to mention the parental, and often perennial, father figure!

Like a stuck needle on a record, these were the tunes that had been playing again and again. I had rejected them, mainly because life experiences had demonstrated that human laws of cause and effect, though perhaps well intended, fell short of explaining the "Why?" of the deepest questions many have pondered for centuries. I realized that the question of why was no longer satisfying and, in retrospect, was serving to block much-needed introspection.

Nonetheless, even though I had intellectually rejected the descriptions of my childhood image of God, I did not do the necessary work of exploring what spoke to me about the divine at that time in my life.

Until now.

It is often said that the universe abhors a vacuum. If something was going to take up space, it had to be congruent with the eyes that were being unveiled. There was a spiritual woman waiting to awaken within. I had seen glimpses of her at certain junctures throughout my life. Yet she couldn't come to be until what was blocking her entrance was willfully relinquished.

In other words, it was time to grieve.

It was time to realize that many of the fear issues that I had had surrounding the Creator had to do with not only harsh, rigid beliefs that I would eventually come to reject outright but also graven images that I had projected onto the Creator, most notably because of the birth father I had never known and the father who, because of his own tissue issues, was not always present. It did not occur to me in the earlier stages, as it was occurring now, that the parental presence I had been seeking had always existed within and was now giving way to something that was not of a full parental nature. I had humanized God, and, based on some faulty beliefs related to early and subsequent life experiences, I had superimposed very limited perspectives on the nameless and limitless one.

Amazing. Surreal. What had initially started as reunion being one of the most highly desired life-changing events (it was, only— as I was now seeing,—not for the reasons initially thought) was now evolving into a journey into the sacred.

Such superimposing was no longer sustainable, not to mention, it was energetically draining. I began to ask myself, "Is this what I have been worshipping? Is it even about worshipping at all?" There had been a certain level of comfort that had now become uncomfortable.

It didn't start that way. As long as I could remember, I had been in awe of and full of wonder about the world. The Creator, as had been understood, existed in everything and everyone. I had had an inquisitiveness about the million faces of God, and nature was part and parcel of those faces. Originally, I cherished the maternal faith of Catholicism that I was born into and having a Jewish godmother to watch over me when my parents were not around. I was able to be a witness to the reality that while both sides of the family often sparred when it came to religious discussions, they never took it personally and embraced each other afterward. Could that have been the potential image to observe when, many years later, interfaith conversations would come to take root, argumentative yet not personal?

This is the memory that enhanced my understanding of the already built-in love of the Creator. And it was from this memory that the biggest stumbling block to opening up to the Creator came to be.

I had mistaken the dogma and doctrine of religion for actually being a relationship (i.e., more letter of the law than spirit of the law), and, in what might appear as the irony of ironies, I once again considered the relationship with the divine as personal.

That might have been fine while still in child mode, but I was no longer in child mode and found that such a relationship was more about growing attachments than cultivating connections. Comfortable though it may have been, it was no longer. The "God in the box" mentality that I grew up with, which was seeing the Creator as a wind-up toy that pops out of the box only when called upon and then grants one's prayer, was extremely outdated. Viewing the Creator as personal allowed me to cast blame for all of my errors while at the same time asking the Creator to pick up the pieces. This was another archaic perspective that was in the process of being transcended. The challenge ahead of me was constructing a new relationship that involved enhancing connections without attaching from a place of neediness—put simply, the personally impersonal sense. Mentor and student were doable, and continually cocreating with the Creator was even better. There was much to manifest in such a dynamically fluid dance, although one thing had to be laid to rest: the punishing parent figure whom I had held responsible for all of my woes, and to whom I had been looking toward to pick up the pieces. And furthermore, I had been looking to this self-created fear-based idol all along. Why? Because I had gotten attached to a particular outcome!

Since reincarnation had spoken to me at a young age, I realized that all that I had as experiences I had chosen before incarnation for the purpose of soul growth. And, as stated earlier, I had also come to realize that the experience of relinquishment had been a clarion call for me to realize that what I had been seeking was not solely external but internal. Historically speaking, and perhaps religiously as well, many of the figures represented from diverse spiritual traditions also experienced themes surrounding relinquishment, loss, and being somewhat of an outcast, according to the turbulent politics of their times. Yet were they really outcasts? Could outcast be another name for pioneer—those who, in all likelihood, saw the bigger picture before anyone else? Moses, Abraham, Esther, Teresa of Avila, Buddha, Jesus, Krishna, Mohammed, and many sages, messengers, and shamans experienced losses of sorts at an early age. Was this experience of loss designed to open one up to the limits of human cause-and-effect-type thinking about what "should" happen and about potentiality? Does such early loss, provided that it is healed, empower one to see a bit behind the universal curtains of divine cause and effect, and thus to connect with such energy to manifest purpose of being?

Many of the spiritual figures throughout the centuries I was studying, now with a new view, had to rely on the soul strength within. Unfortunately, these figures have been idolized, rather than the insights from their profound teachings and ways of being. The "us versus them" mentality of compare, contrast, and condemn has been at the root of worshipping the teacher rather than embracing the wisdom of the teachings. What many have failed to realize is that these teachers, diverse as they were, were also no different from the rest of us in that they experienced the whole range of what it means to live in a human body. What they encountered at some point in their lives was the nameless and ineffable quality within that exists within us all—the pearls of transformation, which go by varied names. What they had awakened to, they knew that all of humanity was capable of awakening to as well.

In addition to starting to see "made in the image and likeness of the divine" from a continually evolving perspective, I began to, experientially rather than intellectually, understand the limits of what is often termed as human love and is often projected onto the divine. This is where the tried and true phrase, "If this relationship is not in alignment, then nothing else will be," also started to be seen in a new light.

The question now before me was akin to a command: Do you trust Me now to let go of what is front of you and walk down a road less well-known and traveled? Can you see that all of your experiences up until this point have been necessary to develop your soul into who you are evolving to be?

Tempting though it was, I could not say no.

The diverse yoga practices, as well as a golden retriever named Angel, taught me well when it came to embodying the phrase "learning from all walks of life." Some poses, like

Krishna's flute, embodied playfulness, something I had long lost and yearned to call back. When studying the Hindu cosmology alongside the yoga asanas/poses, the masculine/feminine aspects of Source energy came front and center. On first glance, I intuited that what many would label as a graven image actually revealed more about the cycles of life, from creation, maintenance, and destruction. This cycle would repeat itself, either in another incarnation or in the present one via life changes. When observing both the statues of Mary and the Buddha, I looked at their hands. Were the open hands of Mary suggesting an unconditional openness to receive and share, perhaps in a gesture of compassion? Was the Buddha, as I had so often seen, sitting in lotus pose, extolling the awakening of the true self? In some poses, the right and left hand met in prayer pose at the heart. Could this have been symbolic of the dual aspects being united as one in the center? Were finger positions, referred to as mudras in some practices, representing the alignment of energy flow in the body, sometimes healing what was imbalanced? It was fun to imagine without getting caught up in any absolute need to know. When I bowed down in child's pose, I thought of all of our Muslim siblings who bowed in surrender as part of prayer. So hard to verbally articulate … yet so soulfully exquisite. The yoga practices found in me a spiritually interconnected way of being and participating in the world and, as such, gave way to releasing any archaic notions I may have had about idolatry and statues.

I could not alter cosmological destiny, and, truth be told, I no longer wanted to. What I could alter, however, were the perceptions of sentinel events—proactivity instead of reactivity. When this shift of perception occurred, so did a significant shift in energy.

For the longest time, it did not dawn on me that many of life's sentinel events were designed to teach me about the grand design and the role I was supposed to play. Many of these events and people who have been in my life were supposed to be there to either teach me a lesson or reflect something I needed to learn about myself.

It's no secret that many of us, often in the name of survival, leave valuable parts of ourselves along the way ... sometimes willingly and sometimes not. We go on, yet there is always a part of us missing. Some of the teachers I had along the way, not to mention relationships, have mirrored such lost parts, which is why I erroneously believed that what I needed to be complete was such relationships! I did not realize that such mirroring of lost parts was actually a mirror of what I had within all along, just dormant and waiting to be called back.

And this was where the energy dynamics of choice came to be.

Up until now, I hadn't really given much regard to the power of choice. Like many of us, I went through the day making choices, and sometimes those choices were made from a robotic state of being. Sometimes it could be called the path of least resistance. Exploring the power of choice layer by layer, I started to see that I had not been fully conscious of just how much power I held in my hands. More often than not, I had given it away. I used to think it had something to do with being relinquished at birth, yet deeper exploration revealed that these habits were neurologically ingrained. In some respects, they were the results of intergenerational conditioning and possibly even imprints from before birth and during the birthing process. This conditioning was no longer empowering, as it once might have been.

Digging deep into cultural stories, most notably the centuries-old story of Adam and Eve, I saw that many of the fear patterns that are ingrained in many of us might have more to do with original choice rather than original sin. The word sin, from its earliest writings, has meant nothing more than missing the mark. Adam and Eve missed the mark, not because they were evil people; rather, they made a choice that came with consequences, not punishment, as have been many surface interpretations. I have often wondered if the choice made had to do with wanting to know all aspects of wholeness in relation to being a fully conscious human being. Such surface interpretations have had lasting detrimental effects of freezing people to stone when it comes to making decisions. Of course, there are many diverse interpretations of this story, and each with something of value to be shared. I often intuit that original choice is what turned the timeless into time and space and that, though maybe well intentioned, the relinquishing of personal power to something external (i.e., the serpent), not to mention practicing discernment and detachment (i.e., doubting one's intuition and getting attached to a particular outcome, as conveyed by the serpent) might have played a role in the beginning of linear time and space. On a deeper level, perhaps Adam and Eve's so-called fall, is, at some point, a fall we must all take in journeying from the familiar to the unfamiliar—only in their case, perhaps before they were ready. Maybe, from another view, this story might have more to do with making us realize that we are no longer mere spiritual infants and that, while we are nothing without the Creator, we are not helpless, hapless beings. There will always be choices, and choosing not to choose is a choice as well.

In realizing that, I also realized that I had been putting chains around myself by permitting paralyzing fear to control my choices at times.

Most of these fears that I had around religion were largely based on someone else's interpretation, often with a heightened emotional tone attached to it. In turn, I had attached someone else's interpretation of my life events without fully exploring what had spoken to me first and foremost. I wasn't interested in shaming, blaming, or even being right anymore. It had been revealed to me that it was now time to consciously exercise the power of choice by choosing something different, and in doing so, reuniting with what was now evolving to be the most abstract, yet far from absent, faceless face of whatever is referred to as the overused cliché—God.

And this is how Judaism came to be.

Alegria, slowly yet surely, began to ascend from the murky depths that had embraced her like an octopus embraces its prey, only in this case, the embrace had been a necessary evil designed to bring her face-to-face with the too-long unresolved stickiness of the past. Once she resolved what she had absorbed and then shed what was no longer necessary, the tentacles of limited perspectives no longer had a hold on her.

Although momentarily drained, Alegria could not, and did not wish to, stop. She scanned the ambiguous terrain, looking for the path of most resistance. The cloudiness that had enveloped her surroundings before she descended was gradually beginning to dissipate, revealing a path that would lead to the next bridge.

The darkened skies of black to midnight blue were giving way to lighter blue hues. Alegria closed her eyes, took a deep breath, and released it slowly. When she opened her eyes, she noticed a sequence of ladders that led to the next bridge. She smiled to herself, noting that the ladders were not there before. Instead of retreating into overanalysis mode, she decided to just be with it and expressed sincere gratitude for what had just appeared.

The dawn was rising. She took a few tentative steps toward the third bridge.

And that was when she was stopped dead in her tracks by the sounds of wind swelling ... which was surreal because it was not that windy.

She was tempted to go into alarm mode but instead chose to breathe through the moment.

And she was glad that she did!

The rustling sounds soon gave way to the sounds of paws

running. The wind, at this moment, picked up its intensity. For a brief, inexplicable moment, Alegria turned away from looking at the bridge. She had seen glimpses of something golden, yet she could not make out what it was … only to now turn toward the bridge and into the lovingly, powerful, knock-down playful embrace of a golden retriever!

Ah … the long-forgotten power of playfulness!

Alegria surrendered to the playful moment, something she had not done for the longest of times. She embraced the big baby of a pup while the golden pup embraced her with wet kisses!

It felt so good to play and to just be, laughing and frolicking with this divine creature who didn't have to do or be anyone special to anyone. This golden pup, with a golden heart to match, simply lived in the moment and simply loved to be.

There was a long-forgotten truth that she had seen reflected back to her from the golden pup's soulful eyes, a truth that had burned into Alegria's very soul.

She would not forget this time.

After an eternity within what seemed to be a mere moment, Alegria kissed the golden pup between the eyes and, holding her closely once more, thanked her for the playful interlude. The pup sensed that her mission was complete and that it was time for her to go.

Alegria watched joyfully as the golden pup, tail wagging still, ran to cross the third bridge, barking all the while. As she looked up into the sun-kissed skies, a rainbow made its presence known.

There was still another bridge to cross, and what awaited her on the other side would reveal itself in time. Yet she had a better idea of where she was going and felt more in the flow than she had before.

And she had been reminded of something she had long since forgot: take time to play ... it's really not that serious!

LIGHT

The most abstract face of God?

Judaism?

Where did this come from?

And why, from its formerly concealed place behind the curtain, did it choose to reveal itself now?

Imagine ... these four questions sitting at a table, engaging both the intellectual and the intuitive. Each side taking turns dancing with the dialogue before them with the hopes, yet not attachments, of cultivating new perspectives.

I found it amusing, surreal, and somewhat disconcerting that in the middle of yoga and breath work practices, something of an abstract nature revealed itself—and in more nameless ways than one. Joyful though it was, it was also disconcerting that, while my perspective on the divine was evolving, I had no practice of sorts, nor similar souls in the immediate surroundings. It was important to keep grounded, not rigid.

True, the energetic practices were grounding in some ways and detoxifying in others. Junk was indeed being ejected out of the trunk and clearing a path for the previous four questions to emerge. Though appearing on the surface as separate entities, these questions were more interconnected than initially realized.

Controversial, seemingly contradictory at times, Judaism had indeed been, and in some respects still is today, the "other" from a historical perspective. Somewhere and somehow in the vast unknown, something was made manifest, which continued to evolve over centuries as a civilization that connects form and formless. From its inception, or perhaps conception, it developed the alternate antidote to the excessive and repressive chaos of the times it was birthed into, times that seem to be repeating themselves today. Far from being punishments, as I once understood them to be, the Ten Commandments were given not only to restore law in the above-mentioned chaotic times but also to ensure that everyone counted. Indeed, it was a radical departure from the times in that it shattered the limited vessel of superficial appearances. The fragments of the vessel—the poor, oppressed, hungry, orphaned, and homeless (just to name a few)—were important fragments that were always part of the whole yet were never acknowledged or respected as such.

At its core and through its continual evolution, Judaism was charged with raising the awareness of respecting the dignity and care of the marginalized other. Yet the marginalized other isn't always an external wardrobe. In fact, many times, it's what appears within that we are so afraid to acknowledge ... and often contains a wisdom like no other.

This speaks volumes that the people who chose, time and again, to accept the Torah and bring the message to the world were, externally and internally, marginalized at times. Sometimes, for every step up the ladder, there were steps that were missed. Equally important, though, those missed steps were ultimately climbed. Turning it over, one could imply that the Jewish people represent every walk of life experience within humanity, and every walk of life experience within humanity has historically been part and parcel of the Jewish people.

And it is that wordless wisdom that has me wondering, What has really changed in respect to the marginalized other today, since the times in which Judaism came to be? The fragments of the vessel that shattered centuries ago still exist today, albeit perhaps in some attenuated formless form. A hungry person may be physically sated but hunger for meaning on a deeper level of being. A homeless person may have a physical dwelling yet does not feel at home within him or herself. What does the external wardrobe obscure? In addition to the above stated, who or what could the other manifest as? The ones who do not conform to status quo thinking and encourage a diversity of perspectives? The ones who experience differently—the energetically sensitive/ empathic souls who often have direct experience of what it feels like to be the other? Could another aspect of the other be the ones who are concerned with the ecological balance of this planet and contributing to its restoration?

One could refer to Judaism as the never-ending story of one people who exists in all people. And the plot time of that never-ending story pertains to transformation on all levels.

As usual, I've dissertated a bit too much, probably because what is meaningful is near to impossible to articulate, but I will try as I go on.

The first question must appear like an oxymoron. After all, who would desire abstract when concrete is, well, concrete? Opposite as these words may appear, I was starting to intuit a connection between the two. The connectedness expressed itself as personally impersonal, a fluid dance that flows like a river— more of a verb than an exacting noun, and not separate from its creations.

Judaism had revealed itself to me as a perspective to my question of looking for the most abstract face of God. At first glance, this was almost laughable. The cherished wisdom teachings of indigenous-based spiritual practices had initially spoken to me first and foremost about spiritual abstractness, though, in time, I began to see a connection between the abstract and concrete. Where was the abstractness of the Hebrew God, whom I would come to discover in Torah, Talmud, and Zohar studies? This God appeared as personal in interactions with humanity then as humanity appears in its interactions with the divine's formless forms today. These interactions included pleading, cajoling, arguing, and more dynamics that appear far more concrete than abstract, and much more personal than impersonal.

But then again, things are not always what they seem to be on the surface. What was starting to emerge was the symbolic notion that what had appeared to be personal on the surface might have actually reflected an inner urgency in respect to evolution and transformation, from striking a rock to speaking to it.

The idea of wrestling with the divine, once released from its gilded cage of feeling that it was disrespectful, opened up new metaphysical pathways. The inquisitive debater buried deep within came to the surface, and with it, the ability to be open to various points of view, even those not necessarily shared. The practice of debate also gave way to the practice of discernment when it came to not getting stuck in limited perspectives.

Of course, being a Gemini, it was also important that the argumentative side be balanced with the intuitive side. Keeping up with yoga and meditation was important. As someone who processes life experiences within the physical body, living solely in the intellect was not an option. Study, prayer, and action, when it was called for, were to be balanced with restraint. At times, this was easier said than done.

For the sake of those reading these words and looking for a more comfortable cause-and effect type writing, I would love to say that Judaism appeared out of the blue. Truth be told, nothing of this magnitude suddenly appeared and kept appearing out of the blue (and it's not lost on me the connection between Jews and the color blue). As stated earlier, there has been more Jewishness surrounding me than I realized. In fact, as I peeled away each onion layer, quite a bit more. I didn't feel it strange since there was a Jewish side to my family, including the earliest beginning of having a Jewish godmother. I couldn't fathom the reasons why people thought this was strange. I had been exposed, albeit briefly, to holiday celebrations and a smattering of Hebrew blessings, which had inexplicably resonated on a primal cellular level. My godmother's mother had converted to Judaism before her marriage, and her husband had converted to Judaism as well. Both her mother and her husband had converted out of conviction. Even now, I can fondly remember a family visit, complete with cousins, when Shoshana (her Hebrew name) excitedly proclaimed that her husband knew more about Judaism than she did. I also remember writing my eighth-grade religion of the world paper on ... what else? Judaism.

As I grew older, I found that most of the people whom I had considered role models and teachers were, in fact, Jewish. Why many Jewish people seemed to be continually orbiting in my small part of the world prompted some inner inquiry. This is not meant to impugn the many spiritually diverse souls who also made themselves present during this time and who contributed to this soul's growth. Nonetheless, when the same old scenario kept showing up repeatedly, I started paying more attention. This scenario became even more pronounced when I discovered that many of my Latina friends were Jewish as well.

As fascinating as the ethnic diversity of the Jewish people was, and still is, the questions I would carry on this continuing journey went something like this:

How did Sephardic and Mizrahi Jews celebrate the high holy days of Rosh Hashanah and Yom Kippur? How were these both similar and different from the celebrations of Ashkenazic Jews?

How did Japanese Jews celebrate the holiday of Tu B'shvat?

All of these questions, and many more, would be the basis of study and exploration ... a little bit at a time.

And finally, the fourth question seated ever so patiently at the table was, Why now?

To some observers, what may have resembled a midlife crisis was actually a crisis of change, which wasn't really a crisis, though it had felt like it. The chronological age of thirty-nine had not only signaled the last year of a decade but the beginning of something new. I had begun to expect more of myself when it came to spiritual growth, while, paradoxically, learning how to drop expectations at the same time. Shul hopping, making rabbi rounds, and taking the formal introduction to Judaism course were now a part of that something new. During my rabbi rounds, one rabbi remarked that though he was convinced of my sincerity, he underscored the need to take this journey slowly. It was not lost on him that there had been some lingering trauma mixed in with this journey, nor had it been lost on me. What had not been reconciled on the yoga mat was being addressed with a spiritually savvy therapist. It was vital to see things with the clearest view possible so that there were no projections. It was also vital to make sure that this journey was not about rejecting any part of my core self by using it to escape the inevitable challenges that life changes continually bring.

Deep down, I intuitively knew that I was where I was aligned to be, whether it made sense or not. I didn't need to convince myself at this juncture with the overused word *because*. Nor did I need to convince anyone else. With the exception of a few close souls, no one really needed to know that my perceptions of the Creator had been shattered into fragments. Nor did anyone need to know that such a shattering had been necessary ... yet. And, as I was soon to discover, some of those friendships would eventually shatter as well.

Nonetheless, knowing that I was where I was aligned to be at the moment did not make this journey any easier. In fact, coming into acceptance, as I would later come to experience, would prove to be a tumultuous struggle, which was even more magnified when I let myself get caught up in the sticky web of excessive why-ness.

Though I had rejected someone else's interpretations of the maternal faith I was born and raised into, I did eventually come to explore the teachings of Jesus and found much timeless wisdom. Hopefully, from a more mature perspective, I saw that the deepest of these teachings pointed not to a personal savior but to discovering the God-consciousness within and connecting with it. The second part of that connection was then putting that connection into action, while being mindful not to cast stones at anyone!

I should mention here that the role rejection played in my life was often negative. However, there were now subtle shifts in energies as gates previously closed were now opening up to other sides of rejection. Some of these sides were able to let me see that rejection, painful though it can be, was much more than the slamming of a door or phone. Though it tended to feel personal, rarely was it ever. I also began to see that rejection and being cast out could also mean being sent toward one's destiny and letting go of all that does not ultimately serve that destiny. For those reading these writings who are connected to adoption and reunion (and even if you are not), this is not a repudiation of pain but rather another way of looking at an emotionally based word, which could not have come had there not been an experience of such losses and then at some point consciously choosing to transform them. The reality was that I was now consciously choosing to reject the neurologically ingrained tunes that purported that one's choice was something that had already been decided by others ... and not the one whose life is the question mark at the crossroads of change.

Choosing something different and realizing that I did indeed have the power to choose was empowering in and of itself. In essence, I was about to balance the role of observer, who was taking action in the physical world to become more of a conscious participant as well.

And without always "why-ning", moving from the comfortable known to the uncomfortable unknown is the underlying perspective to question number four.

Put simply, it was time.

The Torah, often referred to as the first five books of Moses, contains the stories of those encountering the divine presence, as well as the human struggles they experience as seeds of transformation eventually take root. What the study of the Torah also revealed were patterns of human behavior from centuries ago that are just as relevant today.

While I was becoming more involved in the endless and diverse branches of Judaism, I started to be mindful in respect to proceeding at a much slower pace than usual. This was a challenge, since everything was resonating on all levels, yet the last thing I needed was to feel more overwhelmed than was already apparent. Many surrounding me knew of my Judaic studies, Shabbat observance, and holiday celebrations.

Was conversion on the radar? Some wondered. Deep down, I knew that is was but did not speak of it at the time. How could I explain that when I heard the chanting of the Torah, an inexplicable presence filled every space within? How could I explain that the sounds of the transliterated Hebrew melodies, which seemed to roll off this often-confused tongue with ease, not only brought tears to my eyes but made me connect with a sacredness not so easily described with words? Finally, how could I explain that the sincere smiles of synagogue mates at services made a hectic week feel less hectic?

From readings and discussions of those who had explored and eventually converted to Judaism, there had been a rainbow of feelings, from being warmly received to being politely ignored, not to mention everything in between. Given the historical background of the Jewish people, how anyone would respond to someone contemplating conversion would be anyone's guess. I had not experienced any difficulty from anyone that I met … only warmth. Of course, being someone who has had issues with trust, the biggest challenge before me was symbolically seeing the experiences as real and thus embracing them. Was I being seduced by externals? The continued inner trembling and the feeling of "coming home" every time I was in shul were powerful intuitive signs. When a kind elderly gentleman referred to my having a Jewish heart, I wanted to cry, which I later did. Was he referring to something I had not yet seen? This whole journey was evoking such a powerful awe within that it had made me vow not to return to synagogue because such intensity had knocked me out cold.

Yet ... every Shabbat, I returned.

Still, I wanted to stay grounded in the moment. So, shortly after my second book was published and before I boarded a plane for a book-related conference in California, I asked the Creator to reveal signs that I was where I was destined to be.

Simple though the request appeared, it was far from easy. My usual modus operandi when it came to receiving guidance was to discount anything that was too simple appearing. Though I didn't have any clear perspectives on prayer, I was now awakening to a subtle energetic awareness of differentiating between when the ego was making a request and when the request was coming from a much deeper place. What I was now noticing was that when ego was involved, there was usually an attachment to a specific outcome, and when it was coming from a much deeper place, there was no attachment to any outcome. There was also a calmness that came from communing from this place that didn't always come with prayers that were focused on a specific outcome. This is not to impugn these types of prayers, as praying for a loved one's healing was and still is part and parcel of prayer. Initially, my focus had been on making this reunion experience follow my dreams (i.e., one big, happy family reunion) without taking bigger-picture realities into account. Although initially beginning with good intentions, at its core, this desire devolved to one of ego nature. This was true not only of this experience but of many others as well. Looking back, I now realized that my prayers for everything to work out well also had to do with the fact that, being an empath, I had wanted some peace so I wouldn't have to fully feel so much of what was surrounding me—without fully accepting that the sensitive side was actually part of purpose. I just had to learn how to become more grounded within it. In addition, prayer complemented such silence with Creator-based conversations, which engaged more of the intuitive rather than the intellectual.

Bottom line: I had to be open to receive whatever would come this way ... no matter how it initially appeared.

During this flight, I found myself lost in breathtaking views of the canyon formations and snow-covered mountains below. It was difficult not to be sitting in stunned silence of the natural world we often take for granted. This awe-filled scene was even more pronounced over the Southwest, which has had somewhat of a gravitational pull.

In the midst of this surreal moment, the passenger sitting next to me asked if I knew how to spell the word dreidel (a spinning top with four sides, often used as part of a game associated with the holiday of Chanukah). Surprisingly, this former spelling bee champ knew how to spell it. Even more surprising was that this appeared to be a sign of sorts.

The second occurred while en route to the hotel. There was a billboard advertising a Jewish heritage festival for the next weekend! I was a bit dejected to discover that the festival would be occurring the following weekend, yet not so much dejected that I didn't notice some synchronicity here.

The third happening occurred that Saturday at lunchtime. While waiting to be seated, I turned to the person standing behind me and asked if she would like to join me for lunch. After being seated, we started to talk about the conference and about ourselves. During that conversation, I noticed her Star of David necklace.

Hmmm?

Naturally, I didn't want to make more of what was happening than actually was. Nonetheless, this was quite intriguing. I had asked, and I had received. What would become of these messages was now up to me.

When the time seemed appropriate, I mentioned that I was studying Judaism with an intention to eventually convert. Graciously, she shared some bits of her own experience growing up Jewish and in being in an interfaith marriage as well. She remarked that, after much introspection, her son had decided to become a bar mitzvah. Both she and her husband had felt that it was his choice and his choice alone to make. Through her words, I was once again symbolically seeing the power of choice.

She had remarked that, when the time was right, I would know when to move forward. Cryptic expressions and symbols were now becoming the norm.

Upon returning, I was once again captivated by the illuminating light streaking through the midnight-blue skies. I put my journal down, closed my eyes, and listened to the breath ... humbled to be this close to the clouds. True, there would be some loose ends to explore and perhaps even tie up in regard to Judaism once the plane landed. Yet I just wanted to savor this moment.

It had been about sixteen months from that initial meeting with the rabbi, and intuition was now telling me that a decision was coming to be. Since finishing the introduction to Judaism course at a shul quite different from the one I was attending now, the rabbi of this synagogue had started a small group discussion that I had likened to a continuation of the introductory course. Unlike the general introductory class, which had consisted mainly of couples as well as those already Jewish who had just wanted to learn more, these small group sessions discussed many things in depth about the Jewish lifecycle. I learned a lot about what drew people to Judaism, especially at this point in their lives. There were similarities and differences, yet having a place to share our experiences without judgment was indeed refreshing. A conversionary journey is a profound one ... often a "no longer here but not fully there either" experience. Given the too-often taboo of discussing religion, a supportive and sharing atmosphere was most welcome.

Since the Jewish lifecycle reflects all aspects of life, it was not lost on me that confronting the Holocaust and the subsequent birth of Israel was something that had to be looked at with eyes that were in the process of being unveiled.

Naturally, any discussion of the Holocaust tends to evoke the deepest of emotions, as would any discussion of genocide. Eleven million people, six million of them Jews, perished in an event that could have been largely avoided. The toxic mix of what was masquerading as patriotism mixed in with punitive politics, coupled with misguided power and propaganda, sometimes aided by centuries of unresolved intergenerational scars, created an explosive reality. One man was labeled as the culprit, and yet he did not get to where he came to solely by himself.

I've often intuited that the "never again" mantra played a role in the creation of Israel, which seemed to rise like the phoenix amid the ashes. To my questionable and perhaps limited way of thinking, the question of Israel's existence was moot, simply because it already existed. The question before me was futuristic but also contained seeds of the present within: what kind of country would Israel evolve to be?

And this was where I looked at the other side and called upon the wisdom of the adoption/reunion experience.

In some respects, metaphorically speaking, Israel represented the child who was part of both the Israeli and Palestinian peoples, with each parent-peoples nurturing the land-child while ultimately realizing that ownership of any kind is illusory. Each parent-people had suffered a great deal, and yet each parent-people had served a vital purpose in contributing to the well-being of the land-child, who welcomed everyone who lovingly respected its soul, irrespective of ethnic and religious origins.

Looking at Israel through this metaphorical perspective did not diminish the historical heartbreak. I felt for all interconnected sides. I also started to wonder how centuries of unresolved angst manifested in the physical body, some of which I now realize had manifested in my own. Though these evolving emotions were understandable, nothing could change the past. Additionally, I recognized the dangers of foolish compassion, which meant overidentifying with a trauma so much that it justified destructive actions toward others.

Though it was important to identify with all aspects of Judaism, or at least become more aware of them, it was equally important not to overidentify with any one particular facet to the exclusion of others. Judaism had come to represent a celebration of the diverse experience of being human, both particularly and universally. It also came to represent living in the present and contributing to the mending of the greater whole without expectation of reward. In recognizing that, a surreal peace took place on a cellular level not previously experienced before.

And that's when the saboteur archetype made its presence known!

It has often been said that when one becomes empowered, one will be tested. It all started innocently. When a local Jewish educational forum came to town, I was studying the program when something unusual caught my eye: a presenter from Colorado was going to be presenting on the Jews of Spain and Portugal.

This part of Jewish history had been mentioned, albeit quite briefly, during my studies. Though I had grown up with Latinos/as who had identified as Jews (a scant few, I might add), this had not been nearly as common as the more well-known Ashkenazi Jewish population. I listened with great interest as the presenter discussed a historical time in which the "Peoples of the Book" had not only lived quite peacefully in Spain but also thrived culturally as well, only to have it end in 1492 with the beginning of the Inquisition. It was during this time that Jews faced limited choices: convert to Catholicism, leave the country, or die. Many chose to convert to Catholicism while continuing to practice Judaism in secret.

The Inquisition spread like wildfire. The burning bush had indeed been consumed. Many Jews fled from Spain to Portugal, only to discover the Inquisition hot on their heels. Some, upon leaving Portugal, fled to such places like Amsterdam, the Caribbean islands, and eventually throughout parts of Central and South America and the American Southwest.

From the presentation, I learned that while many Jews had perished, many who were not Jewish had perished as well. Many whom we might refer to as herbalists and healers, some of whom were also Jewish, perished as well. Essentially, anyone deemed heretical, irrespective of religious/ethnic origins, perished. It is also not lost on me that many who perished were women, and that this could have been the origin of what would later devolve into "witch hunts" in different parts of the world. Much esoteric wisdom was destroyed during this time.

While listening to the presenter, a cloud of memory surfaced when, upon my first visit to the synagogue I now called home, a congregant, upon learning of my ethnic background, started in on a conversation about the Jews of Spain. I could have read his remark in relation to the ethnic diversity of the Jewish people, which I initially did. But then, when the conversation turned to the Inquisition, something turned within me as well. I could not explain what it was, only that it was more than the typical uncomfortable feeling I was used to. After all, besides it being the birthplace of famous singer Julio Iglesias, bullfights, flamenco dancing, majestic cathedrals, and paths of pilgrimages, what did I really know about the Latin Americans' mother country that called herself Spain?

After leaving the presentation, I could not help but wonder two things. Since I now came to realize that much of Central and

South America had a Jewishness not always openly acknowledged, was it possible that somewhere in my distant and perhaps not so distant lineage such ancestry existed?

And, even more powerfully subtle, could the history of religious persecution presented here be telling me that there was an unresolved issue regarding religious experiences that required resolution before I even considered setting a conversion date?

The intuitive gut was telling me that it was time to resolve this issue and then to move on. It was also telling me that, tempting though it was, this was not the time to go on a full exploration of this particular veiled aspect of Jewish history. There would be time enough for that later. Though I could indeed relate to the experience of living a double life, this was not the time to get stuck in the past.

Yet this is exactly what I did!

It was during this time of wanting to move forward, yet feeling frozen in place, that the centuries-old question of "If the Creator is so good, then why is evil in the world?" flashed from behind my eyes. Up until now, it had been a question I had intentionally distanced myself from, and when asked, I robotically parroted something about free will. As it was now dawning, there was more reality in those parroted words than I had been willing to be aware of. In retrospect, the idea of evil was something I had been too scared to look at deeply, because if I had, it would have meant looking at my own darkness, which was not something I was fully ready to do before these last five years. Looking at evil meant relinquishing some saccharine perspectives that were no longer working. If creation did indeed come from opposing forces, could it be that what has really been called evil is actually more a covering of light? Was evil really, in the biggest picture, what was veiled and what needed to be unveiled? Was this unveiling part of humanity's course correction? The more I studied the Torah and Zohar, it was the partner aspect, rather than the dictator aspect, that was forming in the ethers of consciousness.

This realization in no way served to condone inquisitions and genocides. If anything, it was a clarion call to transformation and the steps leading to that timeless place ... beginning from within.

One of the numerous jewels that had also drawn me to Judaism was its respect for diverse religions and spiritual traditions, even those it did not necessarily agree with. It was because of this perspective that Judaism was never really a missionary religion that actively sought out converts. Though I did not directly experience proselytizing while growing up, I did experience it via absorption in surroundings where it was happening, and it was life-force draining. The idea of some external force dictating the song of one's soul smacked of spiritual imperialism. Religious guidance had been important was while growing up, and intellectually, I understood the need for that. Intuitively, however, I knew that, though well intentioned, that this was not guidance. Wasn't my sacred task to discover and connect with the divine indwelling? It is true that I was blessed with teachers who lived more by example and less by rote dictation. Could it also have been true that I was blessed with teachers who modeled the exact opposite behavior, not necessarily out of being mean-spirited, but so that I could learn to choose something different via listening within? Spiritually speaking, I had to learn to stand up for myself when it came to choosing the relationship I would have with the Creator, without becoming reactive. I also had to remember the divine indwelling in all, no matter how polarized the surface.

This was the wisdom I would have to reconnect with, and it would be far from easy!

These rude awakenings were coming at a critical point, not only in my Jewish journey but in the world as well, when it came to cultivating interfaith discussions and connections. Though I knew that the time was coming to put away any and all angst regarding past religious experiences, a part of me was still resisting.

A decision would need to be made shortly, and before that, a tissue issue would need to be resolved, especially since conversion would mean turning my immediate family into an interfaith one as well.

It was important to give voice to what remained unresolved, and it was equally if not more important to not get stuck there.

A presentation on the Jews of Spain led to the uncovering of an unresolved tissue issue. Unfortunately, in the study of the four-thousand-year-old spiritual practice and civilization known as Judaism, I had allowed myself to get stuck in one aspect of Jewish history to the exclusion of all others. I had allowed myself to become overwhelmed and unbalanced in carrying all of this on my shoulders. When that happened, the rug was pulled from underneath me ...

And the result was a frozen left shoulder.

Alegria was making her way through a forest that was now teeming with life. In all likelihood, the jungle had been teeming with life before, only she had been too distracted to notice. She could hear the roar of the lion as it stalked its prey, which, thankfully, didn't appear to be her! She could hear and sense the vibrational patterns of monkeys as they chatted endlessly while swinging from tree branch to tree branch. In the middle of this jungle, there was a cerulean-blue pond of water. Its waves were made evident by a cascading waterfall partially hidden by tree branches. Like the land, the water was teeming with life.

She walked through this symphony of sound with equanimity and grace. As she walked, she felt herself becoming lighter and brighter. Was this heaven within earth? she wondered.

And, as if on cue, that was when she heard the howl of the wolf!

The howling awoke her from her reality-induced reverie. There she was, standing at the edge of the jungle. With each step through the jungle, the path became more expansive and no longer fully obscured.

The howling reminded her that she was about to enter the next part of her journey. It was not so much a sound of agonal wailing but more of summoning.

Alegria pondered this: what did a summoning echo sound like?

When she stepped out of the jungle, the symphony immediately ceased ... except for the summoning sounds of the wolf.

Alegria froze in her tracks. Before her was a mismatched scene of desert, cacti, and caves intertwined with mountainous hills and valleys, some of which were even green.

And far from what human eyes could glimpse was the narrowest of all bridges. It was this bridge that would lead to her continuing destiny.

She turned around and found herself staring into the eyes of the howling gray wolf. In that visual contact, there was no fear, only love, as well as the deep-seated knowledge that someone's time had come.

The gray wolf ceased howling, and in that moment, Alegria felt subtle earth vibrations from within the ground on which she stood. Grounded in earth energies, she sensed slight tremors, which were gradually intensifying. She froze on the spot while wondering what was coming after her now. Quickly, she exhaled that thought and reminded herself that she had made it this far.

There was no turning back.

After exhaling that thought, she then heard the trumpetlike sound of an elephant standing right behind her, so close that she could feel its breath brushing her left shoulder!

She should have been scared, yet she wasn't. Instead, she was in awe and respect of the creature now standing before her, who welcomed Alegria's gentle hands that caressed each side of its ears.

This was the animal, summoned by the wolf's howls, who would take her to the last bridge.

Puzzled, Alegria wondered how she was going to mount the elephant when she noticed that the elephant had positioned itself on the side of a tree whose limbs were low enough to climb, thus being level enough to mount the elephant.

Which is exactly what she did.

The reverberations of the first symphony eventually gave way to the subtle sounds of flamenco guitars, though no guitar players were anywhere in sight. For a split second, she became acutely aware that there was nothing to hold on to.

And then she realized that she didn't need anything to hold on to because she was already being held.

She smiled within, closed her eyes, and took deep breaths. The elephant was removing debris with its trunk. One journey was ending so another could begin. In what seemed like an eternity of a mere few minutes, the elephant sounded its trumpetlike call again, signaling the approach of the final bridge. When the elephant suddenly stopped short of the bridge, the trumpetlike call reminded her that it was time to descend … so that she could eventually ascend.

The entrance to this narrowest of bridges had a mini-rocky mountain formation to the right of the bridge, obscured by a heavy black cover. Alegria did not know what type of rock formation it was, but she clearly saw something shining from underneath the cover. She also noticed a ceramic version of a raven perched on the right side of the bridge's entrance, as well as a ceramic version of a dove perched on the left side.

She stared at the scene before her, as if in a frozen trancelike state. What did such symbolism mean? she wondered.

And that's when both she and the elephant were struck by a lightning flash of intuition.

Ever so slowly, Alegria and the elephant nudged themselves toward the mirror, and, with its trunk on one side and her hands on another, the heavy black cover was gingerly removed from its rocky-shaped formation, thus revealing a mirror.

To avoid being fully blinded by the light that emanated from the mirror, Alegria turned away slightly and bowed her head low. Direct physical contact may have been avoided, but contact of another kind was forming in the spaces behind her eyes. When the immediate glare had worn off, she looked back at the mirror while holding her hands over her face. She gently moved her fingers over her eyes so that she could get somewhat of a view ... a view that was fuzzy yet revealed what initially appeared to be a formless feminine image.

She dropped her hands and opened her eyes more fully. She then turned to face the elephant and connected with its eyes.

She finally understood.

A mourning period was ending.

What had been concealed was being radically revealed, and what had been held on to for so long was now being relinquished.

It was time to move on.

The elephant lovingly blew a breath, wishing her well. Alegria then rubbed her hands together and gingerly held the mini-statuesque versions of the raven and the dove. Although, at first glance, they looked more opposite than not, they were more interconnected than initially realized.

With concentrated intention, she slowly lifted the figurines to the skies, closed her eyes, and took slow, measured breaths. She released the figurines. What happened next was nothing short of a miracle.

The figurines shattered into a raven and a dove.

Circling each other in figure eight patterns, both flew high into the skies.

A new beginning was in the air!

Alegria was mesmerized yet remembered something profound: miracles were not rare occurrences but everyday happenings that can be seen if one knows how to look via connecting with Source.

The last bridge would be a balance beam of sorts, perhaps standing on one foot at a time. Nonetheless, she was now more grounded than when she had taken her first steps.

And in her consciousness, split-second images of the distinctly feminine formless form, illuminated by candlelight, appeared once again. There were no words … just images of this feminine formless form cradling what appeared to be a vessel.

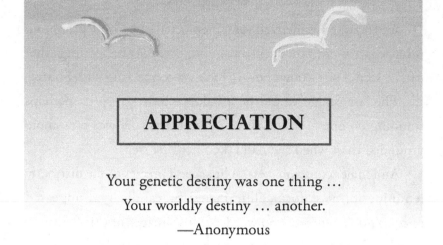

APPRECIATION

Your genetic destiny was one thing ...
Your worldly destiny ... another.
—Anonymous

Once again, tension resulting from an unresolved conflict, coupled with failing to practice restriction, shattered another piece of the vessel, thus creating something new.

A frozen left shoulder!

And the consequences of such an action? Temporary exile/sabbatical from Judaism, with the exception of the high holy days, Torah, and Zohar study.

Truth be told, I looked at what was happening as a time to contract, not out of fear but into introspection, and to ask myself what was really important in the moment. I also needed to take a serious look at what needed to be relinquished.

In the midst of an often-grueling six-month rehab, the above mentioned took on a particular significance during Rosh Hashanah, in which the sermon was on using time differently. There was no doubt I had been using my time and energy in ways that were not always connected with highest consciousness. Though it may have appeared to be quite a stretch to the outer eye, I intuited that there was a connection between the tissue adhesions that were limiting my range of motion spiritually, emotionally, and intellectually and how I was using the time I had been allotted. Such connections were now made manifest physically.

One of the metaphorical images often associated with the high holy days is called the Book of Life, which is said to open at the beginning of the Jewish New Year and close and the conclusion of Yom Kippur, the Day of Atonement/At-one-ment. In between these two celebratory and solemn days are what is known as the Days of Awe. It is a time to reflect on the bull's-eyes, mark misses, and everything in between, while simultaneously gearing up to take higher aim in the upcoming new year. The phrase "On Rosh Hashanah it is written, and on Yom Kippur it is sealed" can often seem threatening as themes of life, death, and the inevitability of change come to the fore. Nonetheless, there is a certain joy contained within each of these themes as introspection asks that one not only becomes more aware of these realities but more so lives each moment in the moment, as if it could be the last. The high holy days also serve as a reminder that we have a lot more power, both individually and collectively, to create the kind of world we wish to live in, and pass on to future generations, than we initially realized.

In short, the high holy days, ancient in origin, can be viewed as living in the present.

Which brought me back to the rabbi's sermon: how was I going to use time differently this year?

Though my primary energies were directed toward healing the left shoulder, it was not lost on me that part, perhaps even more than part, of that healing would involve relinquishing any and all attachments to my birth family and the reunion experience.

When an infant in relinquished at birth, the physical umbilical cord, for all mothers and infants, is severed. Upon birth, a new individual is being relinquished from the former home known as the womb. Irrespective of whether the infant is being kept or the rights of the parents are being relinquished, the physical cord is always severed. The energetic cord, however, is always there, even if the birth parents are not physically present. This energetic cord includes attachments to ancestors, history, and sometimes a lot of trauma that is often acted out in unconscious ways. I now knew that the rite of passage known as reunion was designed to bring me closer to the divine. I had mourned that what I had wished for had not come to be, but now it was time to stand up from that low stool and take a walk around the block. Though a long-held dream had to die, I had not fully died (though some aspects of me that needed to die did). In fact, in some ways, I was more alive now than I had ever been. I was preparing to embrace a new phase of life as well as more evolved perspectives on the Creator. This was indeed a time for celebration.

And it was also a time to ask for forgiveness.

Call me impatient, but I decided not to wait until the Ten Days of Awe (the days of introspection between Rosh Hashanah and Yom Kippur, in which conscious actions can alter fate for the upcoming year). I called my birth mother and asked for her forgiveness for all of the hurts that had verbally emanated from places deep within my unhealed self and had been projected onto her. Until I went to deep places within, I had been totally unconscious about how this experience had affected both sets of parents on a cellular level. I had accepted the reality that, on a soul level, I chose this experience. Yet it was not until I did the work and experienced this scenario from others' perspectives that I could embrace the intuitive wisdom that could not be accessed from the surface. I also came to intuitively understand that relinquishment was never personal. During this time, one of Judaism's most sacred teachings came to the fore. Known as "lashon hara," it refers to guarding one's tongue against slanderous speech. This onion-layered teaching refers to how power and peril can be exemplified in the words we use. In other words, words have meaning. On the energetic level, I have learned, experientially, what many sages of diverse traditions taught long ago and is still relevant today: slanderous talk affects the participant, receiver, and everyone else caught in that sphere of influence. Before becoming completely vulnerable, I had never truly comprehended the sufferings of both mothers and fathers. My task was to understand and accept that it was never my responsibility to fix anyone other than myself and to be present to what was happening in the moment with compassionate detachment and gratitude.

In this sense, this asking of forgiveness and eventual granting of forgiveness would be the catalyst that would allow us both to lovingly close this never-ending chapter via the severing of an energetic cord. This would make space for us to move on as individuals to the new chapters that were waiting with new vistas.

The following week during one of the more grueling physical therapy sessions, the therapist remarked that my range of motion had significantly improved within a short time.

To further augment the healing process, I contacted a rabbi whose practice assisted people who were at various healing stages in regard to grief. From that inspiring email, I designed a ritual of release that involved writing a letter to both maternal and paternal biological ancestors. This letter expressed a plethora of feelings, not holding anything back. Then, toward the end of the letter, I thanked each of them for the wondrous gifts that had been passed down through the generational line—and there have been many! This was essential, as I now realized, in each cell, that I was saying goodbye to ancestors that I would never be meeting. It was a bittersweet moment indeed. I attached the letter to a few balloons. With measured movement, I had slowly torn the letter down the middle, thus signifying a severance of attachment. When the balloon initially failed to take flight, I laughed to myself, thinking that I really had been giving reunion and expected outcomes too much energy! I picked up the letter and tore into it with a bit more gusto. In no time, the balloon, after an eternity of a few seconds, was released from my hands and soared into the skies. I had honored what came before me, even as attachments to it were now being relinquished.

While rehabbing my left shoulder, I looked at other areas of my life that needed rehab. As stated earlier, I needed to reframe some perspectives, most notably how I identified myself. This was another area in which the Judaic teaching of lashon hara could take on a new dimension. Seeing myself as an adoptee, though true in some respects, was quite limiting. The same was also true of seeing myself as mixed-race Latina. True in some respects, yes, but limiting as well. Why was this? Because such labels often kept me stuck in victim-like mentalities, which were another drain on the battery that had been drained enough by moments of self-inflicted cruelty. Reframing as someone who has had an adoption and reunion experience allowed for a much more spacious place in which wisdom from the well could be drawn. The same also held true for ethnicity. This mixed-race Latina was now adding the mantle of Jewishness as well. Yet Judaism was more of a spiritual practice, though I did savor some cultural aspects. In respect to ethnicity, there had indeed been some anger issues about having experienced bigotry so that I constantly distanced myself at times from the world overall. Though my energetic sensitive nature did require a balance of separateness and togetherness, I had shut myself down. Such distancing was now blocking reception to divine energy. I could not control how others perceived me. I could, however, control how I acted and where I chose to put my focus.

In yogic lore, the left side of the body is considered the feminine side, the cooling, calming side. The reality that my left shoulder was frozen told me that it was time to move beyond the adhesions that overattachments to labels can cause. As much as I cherished these coats, especially the one that was about to be added to the mix, it was essential to know that the core of who I was and would be were not these coats, and that when the time came to leave this planet, I would lovingly release these coats.

It was time to start seeing myself as a feminine expression of divine creation—warts, wonders, and everything in between included. That everything in between included more self-nurturing and playfulness. That simple perspective, as mentioned above, again created a more expansive well of wisdom to draw inspirational insights from, rather than always extracting them from external sources.

This was humbling on another level as well. As someone who has been blessed with great health, I had often taken this for granted. In some respects, my role has been as a teacher, yet it was now time to be a student and let the physical therapists and fellow therapy members teach me by their perfectly imperfect examples. When, after a mere three sessions, the most challenging motion of walking my left hand up my back had returned, I knew that all I had to do was to keep working on it, and the rest of the motion would eventually return.

During this time, I saw just how much we take physical motion for granted, as well as the joy of recovering that motion. It was a testament to the human spirit that despair, quite understandable at times, could also be channeled into rebuilding lives, starting with one's own.

Early on in the Jewish journey, I came across a meditation in the Siddur (prayer book) that spoke quite eloquently about the wondrous creation known as the human body. Though initially impressed by those words, I did not let the weight of those words sink in at the time. Up until now, I had simply viewed the body as something to take the important parts of me from point A to point B, no questions asked. Since I had been basically blessed with great health, rarely did I stop and wonder about the marvels of this creation, except when I was not in good health. Even when health was restored, I rarely pondered what had caused the imbalances in the first place. Taking care of this temple was more than just eating consciously and exercising, important though that was. I began to ask myself questions I had asked myself a long time ago but was not ready to answer … until now: if the body was indeed such a marvelous creation and was not a mechanical machine, as was once imparted to me, what was the purpose of introducing toxic talk into this creation?

There was no purpose—none at all!

This meditation opened up into a deeper river of perspectives in health and illness. By profession, I hoped to have been more of a teacher than a preacher when it came to living healthily. Creating health meant more to me than the mere absence of physical disease. While preventative lifestyle tips and the practice of them most certainly contribute to person's overall health, most of these tips concentrate solely on the physical aspect to the exclusion of other factors. For example, what good does eating organic, exercising, and practicing yoga and meditation serve if one is holding onto punitive grudges? Words do have energy behind them, and toxic talk often becomes the barrier to making life-nurturing and sustaining choices and changes.

This meditation also reconciled something that had been nagging at me for years: what could possibly be the source/

sources of illness? Truth be told, I would never know, as this question would cascade into more questions. Illness was not a one-size-fits-all scenario. Environment, genetics, past-life influences, and tikkune might all play a part. What was changing, however, was that I no longer viewed illness in polarized views, nor did I relate to warlike views that seemed to arise whenever illness or the topic of illness came up. Being proactive did not necessarily have to equate to battlefield extremism. Perhaps there was a deeper meaning to illness that was unavailable to mainstream eyes yet possibly available to spiritually astute eyes. I did, however, know this: illness was not a punishment.

In some veins, illness could be seen as a potential conduit that opened the way for proactive introspection and potential restoration to health, whatever formless form that restoration would take. Looking at illness through this lens did not exclude the often painful and heartbreaking aspects that accompany illness. Such heartbreak can lead to the awakening of one's compassionate nature.

Historically, the term "stiff-necked" has been used to describe the Jewish people, and sometimes quite negatively. Yet, as with most everything, there were onion-layered meanings here, and some of them came in the form of sages Hillel and Shammai. Both of these sages debated everything under the sun, disagreed time and again, and yet respected each other. In Spanish, the phrase *"Mejor es doblar que quebrar"* loosely translated means it is better to bend than break. It's quite possible that these two sages were demonstrating bending via the understanding and appreciation of another's perspectives while not breaking into a view that did not speak to one's intuitive evolving wisdom. This not breaking was not necessarily about selfishness or stubbornness; though, depending on the circumstances, it could be. Is it possible that these sages understood the inherent dangers of being too much of a people pleaser, not to mention the consequences of unconsciously surrendering one's personal power?

Yes, I'm being repetitive here.

As I studied these two figures a bit more in depth, the stiff neck may have had an energetic component as well. Though it was the left shoulder that was moving from a once-frozen range of motion to a gradual expansive range of motion, I realized that the shoulder is not far from the neck. In addition to getting stuck in the past, I had also gotten stuck by carrying too much self-righteousness and not seeing with a more expanded range of motion. I also came to realize (continually!) that, in addition to carrying things not my own, I was living too much in my head without the balance of heart. Carrying this was not only limiting but exhausting as well. On deeper reflection, I had been more interested in being heard throughout my life, and when that didn't happen, the pendulum swung the other way. Caring about being right all the time didn't create positive, sustainable energy. In fact, it created quite the opposite. Reflections revealed that I was getting to the root of an interconnected issue involving religious persecution. If I was always in defensive mode about my choices, especially in choosing Judaism, then how could I be a cocreator in the life that was newly emerging? This was but another example of relinquishing personal power by being overly concerned with what everyone else was doing or thinking. It was not my place to be a doormat, and it was not my place to react to others' perceptions, real and imagined. It was my place, however, to see and honor everyone as made in the divine image and to keep detaching from that which no longer served divinely-inspired range of motion.

And speaking of divinely-inspired range of motion, I received confirmation regarding a pebble that had been thrown into the water a few months ago: I was selected to be a presenter at the American Adoption Congress Conference. There were book readings and a book signing, but more often than not, I was not really present to it. This ongoing spiritual journey had changed me, so much that what I had written about adoption and reunion was no longer relevant. Nonetheless, this was not a time for recrimination. It was a time for joy and celebration. I had written about a transformative and traumatic experience, and not solely from the I, me, and mine point of view. The magnitude of processing and releasing long-buried feelings was intensely unquantifiable. In Judaic terms, perhaps this journey might also be, in metaphorical and albeit ambiguous terms, what is referred to as "the right hand of God."

Now it was time to balance the right hand of God with the left hand of God.

And this conference would be the place to begin making that transition.

Though many attachments had been relinquished to what

could now be called the dead-on-arrival story, so that more expansive realities could be embraced, I was now quite interested in learning what the adoption and reunion experience was like for men, homosexuals, bisexuals, and others who hailed from foreign lands. And, in the process, I came across male adoptees, birth parents, adoptive parents, and professionals who were on similar and unique healing journeys.

Not that it mattered too much now, but I still found it surreal that the many I gravitated toward at this conference, like the year before, happened to be Jewish.

Yet it wasn't about whether a conference attendee was Jewish or not. Nonetheless, I could see the spirit of Tikkun Olam emerge in everyone who shared a vision of adoption/reunion/ assisted reproductive technologies that were committed to restoring a more soundly ethical foundation than the one that I and many others experienced during the choke chain repressive era of the sixties. Part of that correction involved educating those about the intertwined gains and losses that come with adoption: the reality that no one can replace another, the importance of grieving losses, and how awareness in adoption practices benefits all. Above all, how the honoring of one's heritage via the sharing of age-appropriate history does not have to divide families but can actually serve to bring them closer. In listening to the latest research by pioneering professionals specializing in neurological health, I felt a new compassion for my parents for the extremely challenging task of raising a child with only scant pieces of the ancestral and health history puzzle available.

On the last day of the conference, and in a small informal

circle, I shared the experience of not only meeting members of my birth family but of also accepting relinquishment to them as well. This was no longer about blame and shame but rather owning one's own projections instead of inflicting them on others. It was recognizing the destructive us-versus-them mentality and taking the steps to mend that inner rift. Part of that mending involved descending into the depths and facing that which had been previously repressed in the name of survival ... yet had been insidiously eating away at the foundation within. All of my parents and ancestors were not just mine in the ownership sense of the word, nor were they just labels of parents and ancestors either. They were people who had lived in a different time, some in a different country, and who had their own individual dreams and struggles. It was during this conference that I fully relinquished the "solely mine" aspect with which I originally saw those who came before me and those who surrounded me on a daily basis. I realized that while many reunions were not necessarily designed to have the happily-ever-after ring, it was up to each and every one of us to create our own ongoing happily ever after. There are many reasons why a post-reunion relationship might not take root, which means if such a relationship is not meant to be, it is vital to end the relationship with as much compassion and equanimity as possible.

I ended the presentation with words of wisdom from the interfaith rabbi, whose blunt candor hit the mark: meditation, yoga, service to others. Indeed, we had all meditated together, practiced yoga, and were more in service to each other than initially realized. When I finished, something deep within me lifted, as if I had finally connected with how to use my books and experiences for what they were originally designed for—a greater good.

Though the presentation was well received, it had been more important to create a space where participants could share their innermost perspectives without feeling judged or criticized. Needless to say, there was a lot of rawness in that room. I trusted that our small group provided an energetically nurturing circle so that everyone could be still when necessary, and then move forward in their respective healing journeys.

On the way to the airport, I shared a cab with a conference attendee who professed a lifelong attraction, and subsequent conversion, to Judaism, which had been detailed in her reunion memoir. When I shared that there appeared to be a Mikvah (body of flowing water) in my immediate future, the conversation became even more animated. She walked a fine line between being encouraging and not too encouraging, which I greatly appreciated. I could not wait to read her book.

By this time, my shoulder had made a full (or what I called full) recovery, and I was preparing to celebrate the holiday of Shavuot, which recalls the giving of the Torah at Mount Sinai. This holiday was also wonderfully surreal in that it fell on my birthday, June/Sivan the seventh. Barely six weeks earlier, the holiday of Passover, which recounted the Israelites' liberation from slavery and eventual exodus from Egypt, was celebrated. Festive though both holidays were, there was a real solemnity underlying them, both particularly and universally. A few weeks before the holiday of Shavuot, a telltale dream appeared. In the dream, I was getting on a very slow-moving bus that frequently stopped to let passengers off. For reasons unknown, I was sitting on top of the bus and noticed that no other passengers were getting on. Eventually, the bus started to pick up speed. I had not been paying much attention … until I noticed that the bus was about to blast off into outer space. Sitting on top of the bus, I noticed a pond of cerulean-blue water suddenly appearing out of nowhere. There was nothing to hold on to, and it looked like the bus was about to crash into the pond! I could not do anything but be with what was about to happen.

At the very last minute, the bus slammed on its brakes, and I was thrown from the bus top into the flowing water. Suspended into midair for fraction of an eternal second, not to mention feeling like a dangling participle hovering over this flowing water, I heard a distinct voice saying, quite playfully, "I hope you know how to swim."

When I woke up, I realized the dream's metaphorical significance: The passengers represented the baggage that had been released during this journey. The bus represented the vehicle for energy flow, which would flow more smoothly without the excess baggage. Sitting on top of the bus represented seeing myself from an evolving higher perspective. The cerulean-blue waters, well … it was time to immerse myself within the life-giving waters and be born anew.

A decision had indeed been made!

Since Shavuot involved the giving, receiving, and, in some respects, the continual receiving of the Torah, part of the evening involved quiet time in the sanctuary with L'Dor Vador (loosely translated as the passing of the Torah and all that comes with it from generation to generation). The Torah, in all of its splendor, was passed from participant to participant. During my studies, there had been opportunities to hold the Torah, but I had declined. I had felt that the time was not yet right.

That night, however, it was.

When the Torah was passed to me, I held it gingerly, like an ancient and newborn baby that evolves. I tilted my head so that the left ear could listen to its celestial wisdom. This was a treasured moment, and in the sacred space of that wordlessness, an already-made decision was inscribed within the heart.

Six months later, after rearranging my work schedule to become more Shabbat conscious, I met with the rabbi once again and shared updates of the journey. In direct parlance, I also stated that it was time to take this journey to the next level.

I was blessed with a rabbi who listened unconditionally to all of the twists and turns of this journey, so much so that had I been in her shoes, I would have lovingly kicked myself out to the curb at times. What may have looked like drama on the surface actually revealed much deeper perspectives. She had seen underneath the surface and into a depth not so easily spoken. I mentioned that I had wanted to release past baggage, lest I drown in the sacred waters. Being human, there would always be baggage of sorts in the present moment, but what I had been consciously carrying around had to be relinquished. Thankfully, now it had been.

She understood completely and greeted the moment with quiet joy.

During that time in the sanctuary, images of Havdalah came to me. Technically speaking, Havdalah is the ritual that officially ends the Sabbath and separates the Sabbath day from other days. After a series of blessings of spices, a candle, and wine, the candle is then extinguished in the wine. Since candlelight has often been metaphorically associated with the Creator, this extinguishing may seem troublesome, as if to imply the extinguishing of the Creator. In that moment, I recalled the lore of the Lamed Vavniks, those anonymous souls numbering thirty-six who, because of their selfless actions, work to maintain the planet from crushing destruction. What this ritual came to signify in that moment was the celebration and connection of such moments without getting too attached to them. There was an alchemy of sorts in this ritual, and indeed it was a partnered effort.

Once it looked like Judaism was going to be standing with me under the chuppah (wedding canopy), I intuited that excessive fear, if given enough energy, can take on a life of its own. Such fear, though understandable, did not need to be incessantly dwelling within this Tree of Life. Radical though this spiritual journey was, and in some respects always would be, others' ungrounded fears of a place called hell was just that—ungrounded fears. Hell was not necessarily a geographical place; rather it was a state of awareness (or perhaps lack of awareness). I was aware of the necessity of descending into hell in order to continually heal. And I was also aware of the hell I created when I failed to act with loving-kindness, for both others and myself. The hellish effects I had suffered most from were when I did not fully trust the Creator. It was imperative now to live from that place of seeing, really seeing, the divine in all, even if I didn't share theological perspectives. This newly evolving wisdom didn't mean tolerating disrespect. Quite the contrary, it meant addressing issues proactively, and not solely for myself either. Embracing Judaism meant, paradoxically, embracing more expansive realities about the many faces of God. In some respects, both metaphorically and metaphysically, those many faces would be accompanying me on the walk to the chuppah ... and lovingly standing back as I took those last few steps on my own.

Resolving the centuries-old us-versus-them mantra wasn't necessarily a reflection of external struggles but rather an internal one. One of my favorite stories tells of a sage who cautions his students that upon meeting the Creator, they will not be asked whether they were a good Moses but rather a good whatever that person's name is. Could one of the underlying themes here have to do with the uselessness of comparisons? After all, the biblical figures had their unique destinies to fulfill, and we each have ours. There are similarities, after all; common humanity and breathing the same air connects us. Yet there are also differences, which, instead of being embraced, have unfortunately been used to divide. One's unique spark is not the same as another's, yet both are valuable. On another level, I found that this tale speaks to the incessant need many of us have to fit in and be accepted—whatever the cost (Rabbi David A. Cooper, *God Is a Verb: Kabbalah and the Practice of Mystical Judaism*, Riverhead Books, 1997, p. 122).

This was a heightened time of excitement, awe, and nervousness. The date of conversion was to take place a week before the holiday of Purim, when this journey officially began in earnest.

That was three short months from now. My assignment was now to study Hebrew names, meditate on their meanings, and finally select two that resonated.

The act of naming has significant power, and the name one holds has significant power as well. Up until this journey, I had never really pondered the significance of names and naming, especially since the name I had been given at birth, and later by my parents, understandably, was not of my choosing. Through Torah and Zohar studies, not to mention experiential learning, I got a much better picture of its significance.

As someone who has danced between being part of a crowd and standing on the outside looking in (and who now treasures that outsider position), the biblical heroine of the holiday of Purim, Esther, was one of the names I selected. It is true that my cherished childhood friend is also named Esther. Traditionally, the bare-bones story recounts a young orphan who eventually becomes a queen that foils a Jewish eradication plot masterminded by the king's advisor, who is ultimately masterminded by plot far greater than himself. On the surface, no one would have suspected that a serene maverick would be the heroine of the day. After all, she appears in the shadows while the action is occurring. Yet, is she really hiding? Or is she just biding her time to reveal herself and the role she is to play ... when time reveals itself to be? There is a quietly powerful humility here. Having been raised by her uncle Mordechai, she has known both sides of the intertwined braids of hardships and joy, as well as being able to see beyond surface appearances. I intuit that she has intimations of her divinely inspired purpose, though somewhat ironically, the word God is never mentioned in this particular story.

It is this last statement that, paradoxically, makes its mark. Does the word God have to be mentioned to make Itself known? On a deeper level, could this story be speaking more of intuition in sensing one's connection to the Creator, and thus connecting to such purposes without necessarily needing to use the word God as an attachment of sorts?

Don't get me wrong—the various names of God have a strikingly beautiful resonance, especially when being chanted. Nonetheless, the fact that the word God is not mentioned in the Purim story could point to the reality that it was silence, away from external hustle and bustle, albeit briefly, that may have allowed for a more soulful connection with the Creator. Such an act of moving away from noise to connect with the Creator, not to mention fasting, required a lot of trust on her part, and this is what the story came to represent to me: trust in divine connections. Though I am no Hebrew scholar, the word that comes close to what I am describing in the connection would be teshuvah. I was now returning and being reconnected with that trust.

Esther embodies a quiet, introspective strength, resilience, and trust, resembling, at least to this partially biased soul, aspects of the divine feminine.

On another note, I strongly intuited that Esther was also an energetically sensitive and empathic soul.

The second name I chose to complement and perhaps, in some ways, contrast Esther was Isabel. In some translations, Isabel means "God's promise." Hmmm? What onion-layered perspectives could this particular name have? Was the word promise meant to ensure one that the Creator is everywhere and within everyone, so no fear is to be had? Did the name come to represent the Creator promise that, come what may, the one who embodies this name will spiritually grow in the face of all challenges and adversities—and through such growth will have sharing potential in unprecedented ways? Did I see myself at this moment in this way? In some respects, I was already there. True, I didn't want to become overly egotistical about the creative talents I had been blessed with, and I didn't want to have a false humility about them either, which was just as toxic. I could no longer not fully acknowledge and embrace them. The creative talents I had been blessed with were to be used in service to life, and sometimes I had been doing just that. More often than not, however, I had been hiding, not wanting to offend anyone … while offending myself.

Well, no more.

I chose Isabel based on the mystical storytelling genius of my favorite Chilean author, Isabel Allende, and also because of her extraordinary journeys that manifest in her writings and how she uses her experiences for something greater than herself. It is through her writings that I have been able to embrace all of my life experiences as far more empowering, not just as a person engaged in a mending process but also as a woman now fully tapping into her well of wisdom. Thanks to her selfless sharing, my soul had been rekindled, especially in coming to term with my personal power. With this promise comes a greater promise to use the wisdom of adversity to contribute to a greater good.

Esther ... a serene maverick. Isabel ... a maverick serene. Both different and yet embodying the divine feminine, which is continually awakening.

On March 2, 2012, in the presence of the rabbi, the director of religious education, and a good friend, I shared particular aspects of this journey, albeit quite nervously. After all, though people can talk about a Beit Din (House of Judgment) and what it can entail, this was something new I was experiencing for the first time. It had been almost four years ago since I had emailed a total stranger with details about a life-changing experience, thus forcing me to take a look at my spiritual practice and a lack of full engagement with it. And now, I sat in front of total strangers, who were never really strangers but teachers assisting with compassionate detachment as I chose to take the steps in crossing a new bridge. I recalled a song about moving forward, backward, and forward (which applied here) and all of the twists, turns, stumbles, and risings. Though it had been quite difficult to articulate in exact words what had drawn me to Judaism, the few words I was able to manage seemed to hit the mark, probably because the arrows were not weighted down anymore. Like Jacob, I had done my fair share of wrestling and would probably do it again. Only this time, love, not ungrounded fears, would be the motivations for such wrestling. Though there were many Jewish people and experiences surrounding me from early on, choosing Judaism was an act of free will. And since Judaism is a spiritual practice of lifelong learning, I would indeed have fun exploring how to live the Jewish practice creatively and proactively.

Connection had been reestablished.

Before the Beit Din ended, I shared with the group some yearbook wisdom that had been written by my former tenth-grade religion teacher a few days before my high school graduation. After wishing me well, she stated, quite cryptically: "In the future, find happiness and sorrow ... learn from both."

I had been too immature at the time to appreciate the wisdom behind those words. Now, standing on the verge of a new threshold and appreciating everything that had brought me to this moment, I cherished that wisdom from so long ago.

On that day, I surrendered to vulnerability and submerged myself in a small body of flowing water in an Edenesque atmosphere, preparing to be born anew. The first two immersions were like contractions as the rabbi guided my voice on the recitation of the Hebrew prayers for immersion. On that last and final immersion, I sensed the welcoming energies of Sarah, Rebecca, Rachel, Leah, Deborah, Tamar, and Miriam in the water. And then, with the breath of the Creator at the crown of the head, and sages assisting at the shoulders, Esther Isabel emerged from the womb-like waters ... a spiritually grown infant woman. Her first cries were of the Shehecheyanu, the blessing of joy and gratitude for bringing us all to this moment.

An emergence of wholeness and holiness.

There had been a rebirth. There had been a wedding, and now there was the shattering of a glass. In the ethers of consciousness, all narrow bridges that had been crossed, leading to this moment, were shattered.

FORWARD, BACKWARD, AND THEN FORWARD AGAIN

In some Midrashic lore, (loosely translated as commentaries on biblical stories/perspectives), the gilgul refers to all of the souls embodied physically and those waiting to be embodied in physical form who stood at Mount Sinai, just waiting for that time in which the wisdom of the Torah was to be received.

Though the concept of the gilgul has meanings that extend far beyond the scope of these writings (i.e., for starters, reincarnation), I've often wondered if the gilgul has more inclusivity experience-wise, especially as it relates to conversion. Looking at the biblical figure Ruth, whose familial origins were diametrically in opposition to the evolving monotheistic practices of Israel, and who converted after her Jewish husband died, could she be of one example of the gilgul experience?

In conversional parlance, the gilgul has been referred to as one whose soul has been misfiled into another vessel and whose internal resonance of Judaism/Jewish practice ultimately culminates in conversion. A child, upon adoption by Jewish parents and conversion to Judaism, consciously chooses Judaism at the age of twelve or thirteen. A long time ago, someone was born Jewish and through external, often traumatic circumstances was separated from Judaism. Then, after a long and arduous spiritual journey, they reconnect with the Jewish people and practice via conversion. Perhaps that soul destined for Judaism had to sojourn and wander in the least likely of all places—and not solely in the geographical sense. Sometimes a soul destined for Judaism has lived a life that appears to be the antithesis of anything even remotely related to Jewish practice, yet they might eventually choose to reconnect with something buried deep within, an unspoken spark that burns like the burning bush Moses encountered deep in the heart of the wilderness. The bush that burns yet is not consumed. An evolving spark that ignites when time reveals itself.

One might think that word *misfiled* is the same in meaning as the word *mistake*. Yet, as I mentioned earlier, what if misfiled is exactly what was part and parcel of the bigger picture? Again, in conversional parlance, as well as overall universal terms, maybe it is not only the gilgul schema that is of interest but what the gilgul also experiences and learns in its alternate universes and past and present incarnations, journeys with the potential to contribute not only to the ever-expanding straight arrow of the Jewish practice and people but also to the world. In some contexts of conversion, could the gilgul also represent the diverse whole of the Jewish people, beginning with Abraham?

Abraham (formerly known as Abram) was called to leave behind everything familiar and journey into the unknown. This is the journey of transformation that he and his wife, Sarah (formerly known as Sarai), were called to make, and ultimately, cocreating with the divine, something greater than either of them could initially have imagined. Who would have ever guessed that Abraham, from an initial lackluster appearance, would not only come into his own after leaving the comforts of home but would also father two nations and be the earthly originator of what is known today as the monotheistic traditions?

A conversionary journey to Judaism, or any other religion, is not a one-size-fits-all, nor is it designed to be. There is something going on that often defies the surface lingo of marriage and family, important though those reasons are. It is not lost on me that my conversionary journey has taken place during a tumultuous time in our world's present history. Some of our most cherished institutions, including yet certainly not limited to religion, are in the process of disintegrating, often accompanied by chaos. A new canvas is poised to emerge. Could it be that this turbulent period is asking each and every one of us to dismantle limited paradigms that don't serve us anymore and are thus contributing to chaos externally, whose origins are internal in nature?

Conversely, on the other side is that this conversionary journey is still occurring. This is occurring during a time when people of diverse ethnic and religious backgrounds, many of whom once held clenched fists rather than open hands, are now taking initial steps toward respecting and embracing each other to manifest a greater good, the healing of this planet.

None of this is easy, nor is it designed to be, and we all have work to do in the mending process. Yet it can be achieved. This journey of mine was not solely about coming home to an ancient and new spiritual practice, important though that was.

It was about the energetic healing that came from continually shattering vessels containing outdated paradigms that were no longer sustainable for welcoming a new phase of being.

In order to embrace Judaism, the perennial question, "Does God exist?" had to be replaced with "God is existence," which lends itself to the question, "What kind of existence?" The answer, of course, is up to us. Like many before me, I have wandered through many land mines that have exploded any attachments to the "I, me, and mine" without imploding or projecting. The mines of culturally absorbed perspectives viewing the Creator as one who rewards and punishes was the first to explode. Some of these explosive mines expounded on the reality that I see *all* life experiences, especially the not-so-shiny ones, as having been integral to bringing me to this point.

Fully embracing Judaism also meant taking steps to cultivate forgiveness down to the atomic level of being, on both the giving and receiving end. This did not mean condoning and forgetting, but it did mean stepping into another's shoes, walking in those shoes with compassionate detachment, and then moving on so as not to be imprisoned by toxic emotions, which ultimately serve no one and destroy everything.

Fully embracing Judaism, I came to understand, with great difficulty at times, the wisdom behind when the answer to a prayer is non-affirmative. Early on in my reunion scenario, I saw this wisdom firsthand, though I was not ready to surrender to it. With time and inner work, I began to experience the wisdom that was hiding behind the non-affirmative. Painful though this particular experience was at times, it was never personal.

Spiritually speaking, I had to let go of what I wanted in order to embrace all of the joy that was now coming.

Fully embracing Judaism, I had to see and experience myself as a spiritual Jew who dances between the particular and the universal while standing on front and center ground. Perfection was never what this journey was about—rather experiencing myself as a spark continually evolving. In that same vein, this journey was also about continually and proactively seeing everyone as made in the divine image, which also means, paradoxically, taking time to revel in divine laughter.

Fully embracing Judaism involved experiencing myself as connected to the diverse million faces of God, both human and nonhuman, many of whom selflessly shared their ongoing journeys, thus contributing to overall soul growth as I journeyed forward.

And finally, fully embracing Judaism meant exploring every aspect of where this soul has been while simultaneously realizing the importance of living in present-moment awareness.

The Jewish people, historically and esoterically, have journeyed on many ambiguous terrains and have wandered and wondered on many different levels of being. Yet such terrains have been, and continue to be, universal in all of us. It is to the journeyers (which is all of us) who continually journey on such terrains that I dedicate this blessing to: may all of your journeys reveal your brilliant eternal flame and illuminate this continuing process known as life.

L'Chayim!
(To Life!)

INSPIRATIONAL READING

Cooper, Rabbi David A. *God Is a Verb: Kabbalah and the Practice of Mystical Judaism.* New York: Riverhead Books, 1997.

Diamant, Anita. *Choosing a Jewish Life.* New York: Schocken Books, Inc., 1997.

Lerner, Rabbi Michael. *Embracing Israel/Palestine.* Berkley, California: Tikkun Books, North Atlantic Books, 2012.

Orloff, MD, Judith. *Positive Energy.* New York: Three Rivers Press, 2004, 2005.

Starr, Mirabai. *God of Love: A Guide to the Heart of Judaism, Christianity, and Islam.* New York: Monkfish Publishing, 2012.

Shapiro, Rabbi Rami. *The Divine Feminine in Biblical Wisdom Literature: Selections Annotated and Explained.* Woodstock, Vermont: Skylight Paths Publishing, 2010.

ACKNOWLEDGMENTS

Though I still have a long way to go in becoming more proficient when it comes to learning and remembering names, I would be remiss if I didn't acknowledge the many nameless and named who came into being during this long and often arduous journey. As the saying goes, some came only for a reason, some came only for a season, and some came, and continue to come, for more than a mere season. It's not so much time itself but the gifts that were both shared and received during that time.

I wish to express profound gratitude to my family, who all along knew of the creative writing soul within, as well as the desire to express it in a spiritually profound manner. It is no secret that writings such as these can evoke the strongest multidimensional feelings, and yet everyone understood bigger-picture realities behind what initially appeared on the surface.

To all of the supportive souls at Touro Synagogue, Temple Sinai, Gates of Prayer, and Shir Chadash, who walked a fine line between encouragement while allowing space for the journey to unfold. The journey, thankfully, is still unfolding.

To all of the supportive souls of diverse religions, and those of no specific religion, who came into being to provide insights at crucial points. Without these insights, I might not have stayed grounded enough to finish this book.

To Rabbi Irwin Kula, for writing *Yearnings: Embracing the Sacred Messiness of Life*, for being a visionary voice in cultivating interspiritual dialogue, and for taking the time to journey into the terrains of these writings and share his simple yet powerful, heartfelt words (not to mention learning how to evolve as a seriously funny person!).

To the staff at Balboa Press, especially Virginia Morrell, who wholeheartedly believed in this book project from its earliest conception and, with great joy, guided this project, assisted by check-up staff, through its development stages until it was ready to be delivered.

And last yet never least, the essential life force energy known as the Creator, who, from this soul's earliest conception and lifetime, has blessed me with experiences that have served as a compass to connect with something within and also much something much greater, thus allowing for healing, revealing, and sharing what, at times, has been dormant in this soul.

ABOUT THE AUTHOR

Denise M. Hoffman, whose earthly roots are a culturally diverse tapestry of North America, South America, and everything in between, is an author and workshop presenter on issues related to adoption and reunion healing, spirituality, and energetic/empath sensitivity. She is conversant in both Spanish and English and is evolving in Hebrew and Ladino. She holds both BS and MS degrees in health and wellness and is currently a Personal Trainer at a hospital-based fitness facility in Gretna, Louisiana. She is also a level I Reiki practitioner. Her previous books include *Ocultanto No Mas / Hiding No More: Unmasking Adoption and Reunion* and *Descubiertos/Uncoverings: Growing from Adoption and Reunion* (Rosedog Books 2009). Her current and continually evolving work includes empowering empathic souls to recognize and develop their spiritual gifts, and women's holistic health and wellness, because when women are fully healthy, everyone on this planet, including the earth herself, benefits. These two are largely interconnected.

Printed in the United States
By Bookmasters